Treadir

MW01127017

Intermediate

Matt Harrison

Technical Editors: Luke Lee, Amjith Ramanujam

hairysun.com

Contents

Introduction

Python is easy to learn. You can learn the basics in a day and be productive with it. But there are more advanced constructs that you will eventually run across if you spend enough time with it. These constructs, while not necessary per se, allow you to be more succinct, re-use code, and think about code in a different way.

This book covers many of these intermediate constructs:

- Functional programming

- List comprehensions

- Generator expressions

- Set & dict comprehensions

- Iteration

- Generators

- Closures

- Decorators

I have taught these constructs at popular tutorials at PyCon and other conferences. This book is based on my experience teaching and using Python for many years. I hope you learn something while in the course of your reading. Maybe it will help you in your next task, code review, or job interview.

Cheers!

Matt

Part I

Iteration and Generators

Chapter 1

Programming Styles

Python supports multiple programming *paradigms*. The following programming styles are available:

- Imperative/Procedural

- Object Oriented

- Declarative/Functional

In the *imperative* style of programming, statements are executed to mutate the state. *Procedural* programming is a subset of imperative that relies on using procedures to evaluate these state changing computations. In Python, procedures are akin to *functions*. State for the program is stored in local or global data structures and is manipulated by invoking functions. This is the same style that C uses.

In *object oriented* programming, objects are the main methods of computation. In addition these objects hold program state, and allow mutation of that state through invocation of their methods. Java is object oriented, as is C++. Though C++ can also be programmed in an imperative (read C) style as well — because it is a superset of C.

In a *declarative* style of programming, the code describes the *what* rather than the *how*. SQL, for example, is declarative because it describe the relational algebra for the result of a query. Other examples of declarative programming are XSLT and *regular expressions*, because both describe the result rather the mechanics of calculating it.

In contrast, it is possible to write Python code in an imperative style to join, select, and filter rows of data. A SQL statement would describe the result, while the Python version would describe the process of computing the result — the code that does looping and filtering. Python is commonly used to process XML and text without resorting to XSLT or using regular expressions.

Functional programming is a subset of declarative programming that achieves the logic of the program by invoking functions. Usually, in strict functional languages, *side effects* are kept to a minimum or eliminated. Calling a function with the same input should be idempotent and always return the same value. By eliminating side effects, compilers are able to make some optimizations. Features such as non-mutable state help to ensure side effects are minimal in functional languages. Because functions are *first-class* in Python, it includes support for many functional features.

Chapter 2

Iteration in Python

Sequence-like objects are iterable in Python. Using a for statement these objects can be iterated over. Looping works for lists, sets, dictionaries, and even strings. User defined classes may also be iterable by implementing the __iter__ special method. Below is a loop over a list:

```
>>> for x in [1, 2, 3]:
...     print x
1
2
3
```

> **Note**
>
> Iterating over dictionaries loops over the keys in an arbitrary order:
>
> ```
> >>> for x in {'George': 'H', 'Paul': 'M'}:
> ...     print x
> Paul
> George
> ```

> **Note**
>
> Iterating over a string loops over the characters. If you are expecting a list of strings, but see results as

Note (cont.)

single characters, it is likely that you passed in a string instead of a list of strings.

The chapters that follow will discuss various aspects of iteration, and using generators to iterate as well.

Chapter 3

The Iterator Protocol

Objects in Python have *special methods* or *dunder methods* (double underscore). By defining these methods class behavior can be modified to respond to certain language operations, or protocols. Python has a built-in protocol that defines the process for *iteration* over items in a container utilizing the methods __iter__ and next. This interface was formalized in PEP 234 and released in Python 2.2. Specifically this protocol provides using a for loop to traverse sequence members:

```
>>> seq = ['foo', 'bar']
>>> for x in seq:
...     print x
foo
bar
```

Under the covers, the Python interpreter translates the above for loop to a while loop similar to the following code. The interpreter runs this behind the scenes (so in cPython it implemented by byte code), but the Python version below is useful in illustrating the iterator protocol:

```
>>> iterator = iter(seq)
>>> while True:
...     try:
...         x = iterator.next()
...         print x
...     except StopIteration as e:
...         break
foo
```

bar

The protocol can be described as follows:

- Obtain an *iterator* for the sequence. This can be done with `iter`, a global built-in function, which calls the special method `obj.__iter__` to retrieve the iterator.

- Invoke `next` on the iterator (which is not necessarily the original object) to get an element for traversal.

- Run the code in the body of the `for` block.

- Repeat the `next` invocation until the iterator raises a `StopIteration`. This indicates that the traversal is finished.

Note

In Python3 the `next` method of an iterator is renamed to `__next__`. Here is a Python3 example spelled out:

```
>>> seq3 = ['python', '3']
>>> iterator = iter(seq3)
>>> while True:
...     try:
...         x = iterator.__next__()
...         print x
...     except StopIteration as e:
...         break
python
3
```

Note

The iteration pseudocode is actually implemented in cPython by generating byte code when a for loop is encountered. Here is an example of actual iteration bytecode, using the `dis` module from the Python standard library. The `dis` module disassembles code into byte code. It is not necessary to understand all the aspects of this byte code to understand iteration. For those

---

Note (cont.)

individuals who want to delve further into the guts of
Python it can be interesting:

```
>>> def loop(seq):
...     for x in seq:
...         print x
>>> import dis
>>> dis.dis(loop)
2           0 SETUP_LOOP       19 (to 22)
            3 LOAD_FAST        0 (seq)
            6 GET_ITER
     >>     7 FOR_ITER        11 (to 21)
           10 STORE_FAST       1 (x)
3          13 LOAD_FAST        1 (x)

           16 PRINT_ITEM
           17 PRINT_NEWLINE
           18 JUMP_ABSOLUTE    7
     >>    21 POP_BLOCK
     >>    22 LOAD_CONST       0 (None)
           25 RETURN_VALUE
```

The two byte codes that are relevant to the discussion
are GET_ITER and FOR_ITER. They implement the iterator
protocol.

The Python documentation describes the GET_ITER
instruction as follows (where TOS is the top of the stack):

Implements TOS = iter(TOS).

The Python documentation describes the FOR_ITER
instruction as follows:

TOS is an iterator. Call its next() method. If
this yields a new value, push it on the stack
(leaving the iterator below it). If the iterator indicates it is exhausted TOS is popped,
and the byte code counter is incremented by
delta.

3.1 Illustrating the iterator protocol

The *iterator protocol* can be tried out imperatively on a list:

```
>>> sequence = ['foo', 'bar']
>>> seq_iter = iter(sequence)
>>> print seq_iter
<listiterator object at 0x872390>

>>> seq_iter.next()
'foo'
>>> seq_iter.next()
'bar'
>>> seq_iter.next()
Traceback (most recent call last):
   ...
StopIteration
```

It also works on *strings*:

```
>>> seq2 = "foo"
>>> seq2_iter = iter(seq2)
>>> print seq2_iter
<iterator object at 0x7cfc10>

>>> seq2_iter.next()
'f'
>>> seq2_iter.next()
'o'
>>> seq2_iter.next()
'o'
>>> seq2_iter.next()
Traceback (most recent call last):
   ...
StopIteration
```

Examples could be included for any type that is *iterable* in Python. For an object to be iterable in Python, it needs to conform to this specification.

Note

In the above examples the print statements show that the actual iterator is *not* the same object as the sequence being iterated over. The types list and string have the listiterator and iterator objects to iterate over them respectively.

> **Note**
>
> The above examples illustrate Python 2 functionality. Python 3 would require invoking `__next__` on the iterator rather than `next`.

3.2 Iteration with `StringIO`

In the Python standard library, the `StringIO` class (found in the `StringIO` module) implements the iteration protocol:

```
class StringIO:
    ...
    def __iter__(self):
        return self

    def next(self):
        """A file object is its own iterator, for
        example iter(f) returns f (unless f is
        closed). When a file is used as an iterator,
        typically in a for loop (for example, for
        line in f: print line), the next() method
        is called repeatedly. This method returns
        the next input line, or raises
        StopIteration when EOF is hit.
        """
        _complain_ifclosed(self.closed)
        r = self.readline()
        if not r:
            raise StopIteration
        return r
```

Iteration is a common operation across sequences and understanding aids in avoiding bugs and understanding generators.

13

Chapter 4

Iterator vs Iterable

Python makes a distinction between an object that is an *iterator* and and object that is *iterable*. An object that allows iteration is called an iterable. This object is required to have an __iter__ method that returns an *iterator*, which could be the same object (as seen in the self-iterator examples later in this book) but is usually a new object.

The iterator is required to have both an __iter__ method and a next method (or __next__ in Python 3). The Python glossary defines iterators as "good for one pass over the set of values". This means that iterators are stateful and only able to traverse the sequence once—the iterator is then said to be exhausted.

An iterable is able to create iterators as needed at the start of each iteration. Each new iterator knows how to traverse the sequence.

xrange in Python 2.x is an example of an object that is iterable but not an iterator. The result of invoking xrange has an __iter__ method, but no next method:

```
>>> dir(xrange(2))
['__class__', '__delattr__', '__doc__',
'__format__', '__getattribute__', '__getitem__',
'__hash__', '__init__', '__iter__', '__len__',
'__new__', '__reduce__', '__reduce_ex__',
'__repr__', '__reversed__', '__setattr__',
'__sizeof__', '__str__', '__subclasshook__']
```

Invoking iter on an xrange object returns a rangeiterator, which as its name suggests is an iterator and has both an __iter__ and next method:

```
>>> r_iter = iter(xrange(2))
>>> r_iter
<rangeiterator object at 0x7fdc0f26eab0>
>>> 'next' in dir(r_iter)
True
```

4.1 Counting

Throughout the discussion of iteration and the various means to implement it, the example of a counter will be used. The counter starts at 1 and increments the value returned for every item in it.

4.2 Creating (self) iterator objects

With an understanding of the iterator protocol, it is easy to create objects that iterate—they simply have to obey the protocol. Here is a simple class that counts. The __iter__ method includes a print statement, to better illustrate the point in looping when it is called and show the underlying mechanisms of the iterator protocol:

```
>>> class Counter(object):
...     def __init__(self, size):
...         self.size = size
...         self.start = 0
...
...     def __iter__(self):
...         print "called __iter__", self.size
...         return self
...
...     def next(self):
...         if self.start < self.size:
...             self.start = self.start + 1
...             return self.start
...         raise StopIteration

>>> c = Counter(3)
>>> for num in c:
...     print num
```

```
called __iter__ 3
1
2
3
```

It can also be verified that the iterator protocol is followed imperatively:

```
>>> c = Counter(2)
>>> c_iter = iter(c)
called __iter__ 2
>>> c_iter.next()
1
>>> c_iter.next()
2
>>> c_iter.next()
Traceback (most recent call last):
   ...
StopIteration
```

Counter could be called a *self-iterator* because the __iter__ method returns the instance (the id is the same for both). Most iterable objects—lists, tuples, etc—are not self-iterable, and return a separate iterator instance when __iter__ is invoked. The following code shows that Counter is an *iterator*—in contrast to a list, items, which is *iterable*:

```
>>> print c
<__main__.Counter object at 0x8d1e10>
>>> print iter(c)
called __iter__ 3
<__main__.Counter object at 0x8d1e10>

>>> id(c) == id(iter(c))
called __iter__ 3
True

>>> items = [1, 2, 3]
>>> print items
[1, 2, 3]

>>> print iter(items)
<listiterator object at 0x8d1f90>

>>> id(items) == id(iter(items))
False
```

4.3   Iterator exhaustion

An iterator is meant to be used *once*. When it is done—or *exhausted*—it raises StopIteration. Where exhaustion normally bites one is in nested loops, or trying to reuse an iterator. Looping over nested self-iterators may not provide the desired output. Using the Counter object to create a matrix may fail if the counters are defined outside of a loop:

```
>>> c2 = Counter(2)
>>> c3 = Counter(3)
>>> for x in c2:
...     for y in c3:
...         print x, y
called __iter__ 2
called __iter__ 3
1 1
1 2
1 3
called __iter__ 3
```

What is going on here? It appears that c2 only created one value—1—instead of two. But that is not the case normally:

```
>>> for num in Counter(2):
...     print num
called __iter__ 2
1
2
```

Thinking about this issue in terms of the iterator protocol can help diagnose what is really happening. In the example, two Counter instances, c2 and c3 are created before any looping. The first Counter, c2, is iterated over, so iter is called on it, which creates an interator. Then next is called on that iterator under the covers, which returns a 1. Then next is called on c3's iterator multiple times producing 1, 2, 3 and finally raising a StopIteration. At that point c3 is done iterating.

Control reverts back to c2's iterator which produces 2 at the next invocation. At this point iter is invoked again on c3 (note the called __iter__ 3 output) which returns the previous iterator for c3. Because c3 is already completely exhausted, StopIteration is raised again, and there is nothing else to print.

The underlying execution looks like this:

```
>>> c2 = Counter(2)
>>> c3 = Counter(3)
>>> c2_iter = iter(c2)
called __iter__ 2
>>> x = c2_iter.next()
>>> c3_iter = iter(c3)
called __iter__ 3
>>> y = c3_iter.next()
>>> print x, y
1 1
>>> y = c3_iter.next()
>>> print x, y
1 2
>>> y = c3_iter.next()
>>> print x, y
1 3
>>> y = c3_iter.next()
Traceback (most recent call last):
  ...
StopIteration
>>> x = c2_iter.next()  # x = 2
>>> c3_iter = iter(c3)
called __iter__ 3
>>> y = c3_iter.next()
Traceback (most recent call last):
  ...
StopIteration
>>> x = c2_iter.next()
Traceback (most recent call last):
  ...
StopIteration
```

One solution to this issue is to embed the iterator construction into the for loops. This ensures a new iterator is produced everytime the for loop is encountered:

```
>>> for x in Counter(2):
...     for y in Counter(3):
...         print x, y
called __iter__ 2
called __iter__ 3
1 1
1 2
1 3
called __iter__ 3
2 1
2 2
2 3
```

19

This might appear a bit unwieldy and perhaps counter intuitive. Another solution is to understand the difference between *iterators* and *iterables*. Iterators only iterate once, while iterables can do so repeatedly.

Note

Neither the xrange nor the range function in Python 2.x suffer from exhaustion as neither are implemented as self-iterators. range(x) returns a list, while xrange(x) invokes the constructor for an xrange object:

```
>>> r2 = range(1, 3)
>>> r3 = range(1, 4)
>>> for x in r2:
...     for y in r3:
...         print x, y
1 1
1 2
1 3
2 1
2 2
2 3
```

Both *list* and *xrange* objects return a separate iterator from their __iter__ method, listiterator and rangeiterator respectively. Each iterator is a distinct object and is able to supply the sequence again. During each loop of r2 a new iterator is created for r3. Each of these iterators are distinct—they have different id's—and able to generate the sequence again:

```
>>> iter(r2)
<listiterator object at 0x8db0d0>
>>> iter(r2)
<listiterator object at 0x8db090>
```

Note

As mentioned previously, StringIO implements the iterator protocol. As a self-iterator, it only allows for single iteration over its value:

4.4 Creating an iterable

To create a class, `Counter2`, that is iterable but *not* an iterator it would need to define an `__iter__` method but *not* a next method. Inside the `__iter__` method, `Counter2` needs to return an iterator—luckily the original `Counter` serves this purpose fine. To be pedantic, the `Counter` class will be renamed to `CounterIterator`. Here is the new code for an object that is iterable but not self iterable:

```
>>> CounterIterator = Counter

>>> class Counter2(object):
...     def __init__(self, size):
...         self.size = size
...
...     def __iter__(self):
...         return CounterIterator(self.size)

>>> c = Counter2(2)
>>> for num in c:
...     print num
1
2
```

It is possible to use `Counter2` in nested loops, which was not possible with `Counter`:

```
>>> rows = Counter2(2)
>>> cols = Counter2(3)
>>> for row in rows:
...     for col in cols:
```

21

```
...              print row, col
1 1
1 2
1 3
2 1
2 2
2 3
```

Note that __iter__ was called only on the iterable, Counter2. __iter__ was not called on Counter (or CounterIterator) as there was no called __iter__ 3 printed out.

Why does this work? When rows begins its second pass, a new iterator for cols is created. This is in contrast to the self-iterator case, where the same iterator was used and was already exhausted. The underlying execution is similar to this:

```
>>> row_iter = iter(rows)
>>> row = row_iter.next()
>>> col_iter = iter(cols)
>>> col = col_iter.next()
>>> print row, col
1 1
>>> col = col_iter.next()
>>> print row, col
1 2
>>> col = col_iter.next()
>>> print row, col
1 3
>>> col = col_iter.next()
Traceback (most recent call last):
  ...
StopIteration
>>> row = row_iter.next()
>>> col_iter = iter(cols)
>>> col = col_iter.next()
>>> print row, col
2 1
>>> col = col_iter.next()
>>> print row, col
2 2
>>> col = col_iter.next()
>>> print row, col
2 3
>>> col = col_iter.next()
Traceback (most recent call last):
  ...
StopIteration
```

22

```
>>> row = row_iter.next()
Traceback (most recent call last):
  ...
StopIteration
```

> **Tip**
>
> *Self-iterators* will exhaust. If that is an issue, make ob-
> jects that are only iterable, but not iterators themselves.
> A simple test for exhaustion is creating an iterable and
> iterating over it twice:
>
> ```
> >>> c2 = Counter2(2)
> >>> list(c2)
> [1, 2]
> >>> list(c2)
> [1, 2]
>
> >>> c1 = Counter(2)
> >>> list(c1)
> called __iter__ 2
> [1, 2]
> >>> list(c1)
> called __iter__ 2
> []
> ```

4.5 Iterators can be infinite

A question that might pop up is: why use an iterator when a
function (or method) that returns a list could also suffice? The
previous Counter class might be implemented as a function
that generates a list:

```
>>> def counter_list(size):
...     results = []
...     cur = 1
...     while cur <= size:
...         results.append(cur)
...         cur = cur + 1
...     return results

>>> for num in counter_list(3):
...     print num
1
```

2
3

A list producing function has one potentially big draw-back—it has to create *all* the data in the result a priori. There is potential for running out of memory if a large list needs to be created. An iterator, generating results as it goes, might incur a bit of overhead due to repeated next function calls, but will not gobble memory. In fact, an iterator can create an infinite series, which is impossible for a list producing function.

Here is an example of an infinite counter:

```
>>> class InfiniteCounter:
...     def __init__(self):
...         self.cur = 0
...
...     def __iter__(self):
...         return self
...
...     def next(self):
...         self.cur += 1
...         return self.cur

>>> for num in InfiniteCounter():
...     if num > 3:
...         break
...     print num
1
2
3
```

Chapter 5

Generators

Generators were introduced in Python 2.3 with PEP 255. This PEP introduced a mechanism to create iterators within a single function via a new keyword—the `yield` *keyword*. Iterators, as described previously, have two problems. One, they must track their state within the iterator instance in order to provide the correct elements across multiple calls. Two, if a list is returned it could potentially use consume large amounts of memory, because it is generated a priori. Generators provide answers to these problems by allowing an individual function to both store state and *generate* each item for the sequence on demand.

The `Counter` class presented previously could iterate, but needed to keep track of its state in the instance. A function, because it cannot store its state, has to generate the list at once. What if there was a way for a function to store state and generate the members of sequence one at a time? Generators do exactly that.

The Python documentation defines a generator as follows:

> A function which returns an iterator. It looks like a normal function except that it contains `yield` statements for producing a series [of] values usable in a for-loop or that can be retrieved one at a time with the `next()` function. Each yield temporarily suspends processing, remembering the location execution state (including local variables

and pending try-statements). When the generator resumes, it picks-up where it left-off (in contrast to functions which start fresh on every invocation).

The yield keyword, when used within a function—or method—tells the Python interpreter create an *iterator* from the function. When Python encounters a function that contain this keyword, it treats the function differently. Invoking the generator function alone will just return a generator instance, rather than a function instance:

```
>>> def simple_generator():
...     print "generate"
...     yield 1
...     yield 2

>>> print simple_generator()
<generator object simple_generator at 0x8cbaa0>
```

Careful reading of the invocation of the simple_generator function above shows one of the differences between generators and normal functions. The simple_generator function include a call to the print statement, yet the invocation of generate did not print that out. This illustrates the first difference between a generator and a function—*generators are not executed when they are invoked, only when they are iterated over.* The Python interpreter knows this is a generator (because the yield keyword is used in it) and just returns a generator object during invocation, without executing it.

Note

Normal functions return None by default. If simple_generator were a normal function the result of a printing a function invocation would be None instead of <generator object ...>:

```
>>> def normal_function():
...     y = 2 + 2  # no default return

>>> print normal_function()
None
```

The second difference between a function and a generator is that *generators can be iterated over*. Because the result of the generator is an iterator, it follows the iterator protocol and can be iterated over. When the next invocation occurs, the generator returns the result of the first yield statement:

```
>>> for x in simple_generator():
...     print x
generate
1
2
```

Here simple_generator is iterated over using the iterator protocol. Each time next is executed should have a corresponding yield statement:

```
>>> seq = iter(simple_generator())
>>> x = seq.next()
generate
>>> print x
1
>>> x = seq.next()
>>> print x
2
>>> x = seq.next()
Traceback (most recent call last):
  ...
StopIteration
```

A third difference between a function and a generator is that *generators freeze their state after a* yield *statement*. Unlike functions, which target the contents of their block for garbage collection after they are executed, generators suspend their state of execution until the next next call.

The process of looping over a generator could be described as:

- wait for a next call (looping over the generator)

- execute from start (or frozen state) until a yield statement is encountered

- return the value of the yield statement to the next call

- freeze the state of the generator function

- repeat (note that starting state will be line following the `yield`) until `return` or `StopIteration` raised

Here is a simple generator that implements the `Counter` class described previously:

```
>>> def counter_gen(size):
...     cur = 1
...     while cur <= size:
...         yield cur
...         cur = cur + 1
>>> for num in counter_gen(2):
...     print num
1
2
```

In the looping invocation above, 2 is passed into counter_gen as an argument and the function is iterated over (next is called behind the scenes). When the first next is called, the body of the function starts executing, and the while test passes (1 <= 2). The yield statement is encountered and 1 is returned as the first item of iteration. The generator state is suspended at this point with the local variable cur having the value of 1. The body of the loop is executed and num is printed. The loop then invokes next again on the next pass.

During the second pass, the state of the generator is resumed, with cur having the value of 1 and execution resumes where it left off—at the line cur = cur + 1—not at the start of the function. At this point cur becomes 2, the while loop is true again, and the yield statement returns 2. The execution state of the generator is frozen again, and control is passed back to the body of the loop to print num.

Because for loops follow the iterator protocol (they do not stop until a StopIteration is raised), next is called again on the generator. At this point the while test fails and while block is finished. The remaining code (an empty block—or implicit return None) is invoked. Any return statement inside of a generator is treated as raising a StopIteration and the for loop finishes.

5.1 Function generators exhaust

Because generator functions exhaust, they do not serve well for re-use or in matrix creation:

```
>>> c1 = counter_gen(2)
>>> c2 = counter_gen(3)
>>> for x in c1:
...     for y in c2:
...         print x, y
1 1
1 2
1 3
```

5.2 Generators return a generator object

The result of calling a generator is a generator object. This object has both an __iter__ method, and a next method:

```
>>> gen = counter_gen(3)
>>> gen
<generator object counter_gen at 0x8c8af0>
>>> dir(gen)
['__class__', '__delattr__', '__doc__',
'__format__', '__getattribute__', '__hash__',
'__init__', '__iter__', '__name__', '__new__',
'__reduce__', '__reduce_ex__', '__repr__',
'__setattr__', '__sizeof__', '__str__',
'__subclasshook__', 'close', 'gi_code',
'gi_frame', 'gi_running', 'next', 'send',
'throw']
```

Invoking __iter__ on a generator will return the same generator object instance. Generators are self-iterators!

```
>>> iter(gen) == gen.__iter__() == gen
True
```

Because generators are self-iterators, they are not reusable.

Note

It should be inferred that generators follow the iterator protocol as they have both an __iter__ and a next method.

29

5.3 Generators can be infinite

As stated previously, generators can create sequence elements on the fly. This can be performed ad infinitum, allowing the calling code to determine the point at which sufficient elements have been obtained. Following is an example of an infinite generator:

```
>>> def gen_forever():
...     i = 1
...     while True:
...         yield i
...         i = i + 1

>>> for num in gen_forever():
...     if num > 3:
...         break
...     print num
1
2
3
```

5.4 return stops generation

A return statement in a generator will cause the loop to exit. The following generator will never iterate to 3:

```
>>> def gen_with_return():
...     yield 1
...     yield 2
...     return
...     yield 3

>>> for num in gen_with_return():
...     print num
1
2
```

Here is how the return plays out under the covers:

```
>>> an_iter = iter(gen_with_return())
>>> an_iter.next()
1
>>> an_iter.next()
2
>>> an_iter.next()
```

```
Traceback (most recent call last):
  ...
StopIteration
```

The following sections will explain how generators are commonly used in Python code.

Chapter 6

Object Generators

Not only can functions generate, but methods can as well. There are two common ways to use generators with objects.

One, by returning a generator from the __iter__ method, an object can be *iterable*. This allows an object instance to be iterated over.

Two, because generators are iterators, any method that is a generator can be iterated over. This allows iteration over a method. For example a class representing a tree structure might have methods named breadth_first_traversal and depth_first_traversal that are both generators.

Here is an object, Counter3, that illustrates the counting iterator seen throughout this book. It is iterable using a generator:

```
>>> class Counter3:
...     def __init__(self, size):
...         self.size = size
...
...     def __iter__(self):
...         cur = 1
...         while cur <= self.size:
...             yield cur
...             cur = cur + 1

>>> for x in Counter3(3):
...     print x
1
2
3
```

6.1 Object iterator reuse

One interesting aspect of object generators implemented by
__iter__ is that they *are reusable if they do not attach state to the*
instance:

```
>>> c1 = Counter3(3)
>>> for x in c1:
...     print x
1
2
3
>>> for x in c1:
...     print x
1
2
3
```

This object will not fall prey to the nested loop matrix
creation issue, seen with self-iterators:

```
>>> c2 = Counter3(2)
>>> c3 = Counter3(3)
>>> for x in c2:
...     for y in c3:
...         print x, y
1 1
1 2
1 3
2 1
2 2
2 3
```

Note

Recall that this was not the case with function generators. Because generators created in functions exhaust,
they cannot be used in this nested situation. Function
generators are self-iterators, while the above object creates a new generator instance everytime a Counter3 object is iterated over. The __iter__ method (which creates
the generator) is called during the looping. In contrast
with a function generator, which was created outside of
the loops in previous examples.

Every new iteration over c3 will result in a new generator being created (ie `iter` is called again), so there is no need to worry about exhaustion here:

```
>>> iter(c2) == c2
False
```

However, if the state of the generator is stored as attributes on the object instance problems might arise.

In the following example, `Counter4`, the current value is stored on the instance as `self.cur` instead of local to the generator. (This is not necessary logic, but introduced to illustrate a potential gotcha). Again the nested loop for matrix creation failure rears its ugly head:

```
>>> class Counter4:
...     def __init__(self, size):
...         self.size = size
...         self.cur = 1
...
...     def __iter__(self):
...         while self.cur <= self.size:
...             yield self.cur
...             self.cur = self.cur + 1


>>> c2 = Counter4(2)
>>> c3 = Counter4(3)
>>> for x in c2:
...     for y in c3:
...         print x, y
1 1
1 2
1 3
```

In this example rather than each loop having its own state in the generator, the state of `cur` is attached to the instance, and thus only allows for a single traversal.

6.2   Object method generators

In addition to implementing `__iter__`, any method that is a generator may be iterated over. Here is `Counter5` that generates with the count method:

```
>>> class Counter5:
```

```
...        def __init__(self, size):
...            self.size = size
...
...        def count(self):
...            cur = 1
...            while cur <= self.size:
...                yield cur
...                cur = cur + 1
```

Generator methods perform similarly to generator functions. They are self-iterators:

```
>>> c5 = Counter5(2)
>>> c5_gen = c5.count()
>>> iter(c5_gen) == c5_gen
True
```

As such, generator methods behave slightly differently than _iter_ generators, and cannot simply serve as a drop-in replacement.

```
>>> c2 = Counter5(2).count()
>>> c3 = Counter5(3).count()
>>> for x in c2:
...     for y in c3:
...         print x, y
1 1
1 2
1 3
```

For the matrix creation example to work, count needs to be invoked inside of the for loop:

```
>>> c2 = Counter5(2)
>>> c3 = Counter5(3)
>>> for x in c2.count():
...     for y in c3.count():
...         print x, y
1 1
1 2
1 3
2 1
2 2
2 3
```

Chapter 7

Generators in Practice

When is it appropriate to use a generator? A very basic response is that a generator can replace any function that returns a list. The main pattern to look for is accumulation into a list during a loop. To use generators instead, just `yield` the result at that point where the accumulation would have occurred. As was shown previously, the following two functions are essentially the same in that they both return an iterable whose items are equal:

```
>>> def counter_list(size):
...     results = []
...     cur = 1
...     while cur <= size:
...         results.append(cur)
...         cur = cur + 1
...     return results

>>> def counter_gen(size):
...     cur = 1
...     while cur <= size:
...         yield cur
...         cur = cur + 1

>>> list(counter_gen(500)) == counter_list(500)
True
```

The generator solution is almost identical but there are three differences:

- The accumulator, `results` in this case, is never created

- Instead of appending an item to `results`, the item is just *yielded*

- There is usually no `return` statement in this generator. (Though it can be used to signal exhaustion)

Any function or method that acts as an accumulator is a candidate for a generator. The remainder of this section evaluates generator characteristics.

7.1 Generators exhaust

Unlike lists, `range`, `xrange`, and non-self iterators, generator functions do not play well with reuse. Once they are used, they usually cannot be re-used:

```
>>> five = counter_gen(5)
>>> [x for x in five]
[1, 2, 3, 4, 5]

>>> [x for x in five]
[]

>>> five_xr = xrange(1, 6)
>>> [x for x in five_xr]
[1, 2, 3, 4, 5]

>>> [x for x in five_xr]
[1, 2, 3, 4, 5]
```

7.2 Chaining generators

Another common use of a generator is to act as a filter on sequences. A generator can be useful for a reusable chunk of code to perform filtering or manipulation of sequences. Once armed with a few generators, they can be chained together to apply their logic to a sequence:

```
>>> def positive(seq):
...     for x in seq:
...         if x >= 0:
...             yield x
```

```
>>> def every_other(gen):
...     for x in gen:
...         yield x
...         gen.next()

>>> def double(seq):
...     for x in seq:
...         yield x
...         yield x

>>> seq = range(-5, 5)
>>> pos = positive(seq)
>>> skip = every_other(pos)
>>> two = double(skip)
>>> [x for x in two]
[0, 0, 2, 2, 4, 4]
```

> **Note**
>
> Because the every_other generator calls next on the parameter passed into it, it will only operate on an iterator, not an iterable like a list. However it will not complain during invocation of the generator:
>
> ```
> >>> even = every_other(range(2))
> ```
>
> Because generators are lazy, an exception will occur only during iteration, not invocation of the generator:
>
> ```
> >>> list(even)
> Traceback (most recent call last):
>   ...
> AttributeError: 'list' object has no attribute 'next'
> ```
>
> A more sequence friendly version may be:
>
> ```
> >>> def every_other(seq):
> ...     for i, x in enumerate(seq):
> ...         if i % 2 == 0:
> ...             yield x
>
> >>> list(every_other(range(5)))
> [0, 2, 4]
> ```
>
> or coercing the sequence to an iterator (which is guaranteed to have a next method):

39

Note (cont.)

```
>>> def every_other(gen):
...     gen = iter(gen)
...     for x in gen:
...         yield x
...         gen.next()

>>> list(every_other(range(5)))
[0, 2, 4]
```

Make sure that generator filters such as these know whether they are dealing with iterators or iterables.

Tip

The previous example could be written in a couple of different ways. A single generator could perform all the manipulation logic at once:

```
>>> def do_foo(seq):
...     pos_count = 0
...     for x in seq:
...         if x >= 0:
...             if pos_count % 2 == 0:
...                 yield x
...                 yield x
...             pos_count += 1

>>> list(do_foo(range(-5, 5)))
[0, 0, 2, 2, 4, 4]
```

This code is harder to understand than the separate functions. If chaining these filters together is common, it is cleaner to create the unique generators, positive, every_other, and double, then define do_foo thusly:

```
>>> def do_foo(seq):
...     seq = positive(seq)
...     seq = every_other(seq)
...     seq = double(seq)
...     for x in seq:
...         yield x

>>> list(do_foo(range(-5, 5)))
[0, 0, 2, 2, 4, 4]
```

Tip (cont.)

Adding the composite generator involves more lines of code, but is much more readable. It also applies the *Unix Philosophy* of "do one thing well". A bunch a generators that are one trick ponies can then be chained (or piped in the unix world) together. The declarative nature of the newer do_foo is straightforward.

Note

An alternative *functional* spelling of do_foo nests the generators:

```
>>> def do_foo(seq):
...     for x in positive(every_other(
...             double(seq))):
...             yield x
```

7.3 Debugging generators

Due to the lazy nature of their sequence generation, generators can be tricky to debug. pdb for instance can *step* into functions, but with generators it behaves differently. pdb will not step into a generator until it is actually *iterated over*. If a file contained the following code, pdb would not allow *stepping* into the positive function. If the generator is never iterated over the code will never execute and the debugger will not have the chance to jump into that code:

```
def positive(seq):
    for x in seq:
        if x >= 0:
            yield x

import pdb; pdb.set_trace()
seq = positive(range(5))
```

Only by stepping into the iteration over a generator, is it possible to debug a generator via pdb. When seq is being iterated over in the for loop, *stepping into the loop* will enter into the generator:

```
def positive(seq):
    for x in seq:
        if x >= 0:
            yield x

import pdb; pdb.set_trace()
seq = positive(range(5))

# stepping in here will put pdb into positive
for y in seq:
    print y
```

When the actual iteration occurs a few screenfuls of code (or in a different module) away from the creation of the generator groking the code requires a heavier cognitive load. By keeping generators small and testable, this cognitive load is lessened a bit.

Tip

During debugging a useful way to inspect a generator is to turn it into a list. After each line of the following, seq is just a generator. Because generators are lazy, understanding what is happening to seq by simply inspecting the seq variable does not work:

```
>>> seq = range(-5, 5)
>>> seq = positive(seq)
>>> seq = every_other(seq)
>>> seq = double(seq)
```

By turning the generator into a list, the lazy evaluation is forced to occur. If there was an issue with the positive function the following code might help expose it:

```
>>> seq = range(-5, 5)
>>> seq = positive(seq)
>>> seq = list(seq)
>>> print seq
[0, 1, 2, 3, 4]
```

> **Tip (cont.)**
>
> Just remember that a list will potentially consume more memory. Also a list is not exhaustible, so behavior that occurs following the conversion to a list is not necessarily the same as the behavior with a generator.

7.4 Generators do not index or slice

Another incompatibility between lists and generators is their support for slicing operators. Out of the box, generators do not support indexing or slicing:

```
>>> pos = positive(range(-5, 5))
>>> pos[1]
Traceback (most recent call last):
  ...
TypeError: 'generator' object is not subscriptable
```

Luckily the itertools module, included in the standard library, contains an islice function that replicates a portion of the slicing functionality. Rather than returning a list, islice returns an iterable object:

```
>>> from itertools import islice
>>> seq = islice(pos, 1, 3)
>>> print seq
<itertools.islice object at 0x8f3680>
```

The results of islice need to be iterated over to see the results:

```
>>> seq.next()
1
>>> seq.next()
2
>>> seq.next()
Traceback (most recent call last):
  ...
StopIteration
```

> **Note**
>
> Negative slicing is not available with generators nor with islice. Again, because of possible infinite lengths of generated items, there is no mechanism for starting at the end and counting backwards.

7.5 Generators have no inherent length

Because generators may generate infinitely, there is no reliable mechanism to create a __len__ method (which the built-in len function calls under the covers). The only way to count the items in a generator is to iterate over them. That might take a long time with an infinite generator.

7.6 Generators may be slower

Looping over a sequence requires using the iteration protocol, which calls next at every step. It is possible that a generator iteration is slower than other methods, such as list iteration. Using the timeit module on short chunks of code can help to profile and alleviate timing concerns:

```
>>> def iter_list():
...      for x in [0, 1, 2, 3, 4, 5]:
...          pass

>>> def iter_gen():
...      def gen():
...          yield 1
...          yield 2
...          yield 3
...          yield 4
...          yield 5
...      for x in gen():
...          pass

>>> import timeit
>>> t = timeit.Timer('iter_list()',
...      setup='from __main__ import iter_list')
>>> print t.timeit()
0.5026171207427979
```

```
>>> t = timeit.Timer('iter_gen()',
...     setup='from __main__ import iter_gen')
>>> print t.timeit()
0.8130838871002197
```

7.7 Generators may consume less memory

Because generators are lazy they (potentially) require much less memory than lists when dealing with large numbers of items. If memory is limited and single traversal is not a problem, generators may be an appropriate solution for conserving memory.

7.8 Generators are True

Idiomatic Python suggests that checking if a sequence implicitly evaluates to a boolean is cleaner that casting it to a bool or checking that the length is greater than zero. Unlike lists, where that behavior holds, a generator *always* evaluates to True:

```
>>> def odd_list(seq):
...     results = []
...     for x in seq:
...         if x % 2:
...             results.append(x)
...     return results

>>> if odd_list([0, 2, 4]):
...     print "Found odd"
... else:
...     print "No odd"
No odd

>>> bool(odd_list([0, 2, 4]))
False

>>> def odd_gen(seq):
...     for x in seq:
...         if x % 2:
...             yield x

>>> if odd_gen([0, 2, 4]):
```

45

```
...     print "Found odd"
... else:
...     print "No odd"
Found odd

>>> bool(odd_gen([0, 2, 4]))
True
```

This is an area where a generator is not just a drop-in replacement for a list. Not understanding the *truthiness* of generators may lead to a fun debugging session.

7.9   A non-generator: xrange

The built-in function xrange (range in Python 3) is *not* a generator. Many Python programmers do not understand this and conflate xrange with generators. It is not uncommon to find a website or blog claiming that xrange is a generator. This is not true. They do not behave in the same manner. Here are some examples of the differences.

The xrange function can be indexed (but not sliced):

```
>>> to_ten = xrange(1, 11)
>>> to_ten[2]
3
>>> to_ten[1:3]
Traceback (most recent call last):
  ...
TypeError: sequence index must be integer, not 'slice'
```

The xrange function has no next method. It is iterable but not an iterator itself:

```
>>> 'next' in dir(to_ten)
False
>>> to_ten.__class__
<type 'xrange'>
>>> iter(to_ten)
<rangeiterator object at 0x7f4d669e8990>
```

Because xrange is an iterable it does *not* exhaust and can be iterated over many times:

```
>>> list(to_ten)
[1, 2, 3, 4, 5, 6, 7, 8, 9, 10]
>>> list(to_ten)
```

```
[1, 2, 3, 4, 5, 6, 7, 8, 9, 10]
```

Though xrange is also lazy about sequence creation, do not confuse it with a generator. They behave slightly differently.

7.10 A generator in `collections.py`

The OrderedDict class found in the collections.py module in the Python Standard Library uses a generator in its __iter__ method:

```
class OrderedDict(dict):
    ...
    def __iter__(self):
        'od.__iter__() <==> iter(od)'
        # Traverse the linked list in order.
        NEXT, KEY = 1, 2
        root = self.__root
        curr = root[NEXT]
        while curr is not root:
            yield curr[KEY]
            curr = curr[NEXT]
```

Because very minimal state is stored in the __iter__ method, it can be used to create a matrix. (Altering self.__root before the second iteration loop would mess up the iterator, but given that there are two underscores before the attribute, it would probably be best to leave that implementation detail alone):

```
>>> from collections import OrderedDict
>>> d = OrderedDict()
>>> for i in range(1, 4):
...     d[i] = i
>>> for x in d:
...     for y in d:
...         print x, y
1 1
1 2
1 3
2 1
2 2
2 3
3 1
3 2
```

3 3

Chapter 8

List or Generator?

Given all the similarities and differences between lists and generators it may be confusing to determine when to use one or the other. Here are some rules to decide which is appropriate.

Note

In Python 3 many of the iteration semantics have become more lazy. For example the `range` built-in in Python 3 is essentially what `xrange` was in Python 2. Remember that `xrange` is *not* actually a generator, but just has lazy, on-the-fly semantics similar to generators. Functions such as `zip` are also lazy in Python 3. To get the previous Python 2 behavior, wrapping with `list` may be necessary.

8.1 Repeated use of data

If access to items in a sequence is needed repeatedly, a generator alone cannot provide that access. In such situations non-exhaustible iterables such as a list—or converting a generator to a list—may be a better choice.

8.2 Data fits into memory

If the complete sequence fits into memory, a list may prove to be a slightly faster choice than a generator. Remember that the repeated function overhead invoked for every item in the sequence does not come for free. Using the `timeit` module may help to alleviate such concerns.

8.3 Operating on the sequence

If operations on the whole sequence need to be performed, such as `len`, or `reversed`, a generator is probably not the right choice. While `len`, or `sorted` will work on a non-infinite generator, `reversed` will fail:

```
>>> reversed(counter_gen(5))
Traceback (most recent call last):
  ...
TypeError: argument to reversed() must be a sequence
```

8.4 Conversion between lists and generators

A list can always be converted into a generator. The reverse is *not* true—remember generators can be infinite. Here is function to perform conversion of a sequence (or list) to a generator:

```
>>> def identity_gen(seq):
...     for x in seq:
...         yield x
```

The built-in `list` function is useable given non-infinite generators and sufficient momery when the conversion from generator to list is needed:

```
>>> [0, 1] == list(identity_gen([0, 1]))
True
```

8.5 Python is becoming more lazy

A trend of Python 3 is laziness. For example the keys method of a dictionary in Python 2 returned a list of keys, whereas in Python 3 it returns a "set-like object providing a view of the dictionary's keys". The migration of the behavior of range follows suite. PEP 3106 discusses this in more detail. An interesting facet of these *views* is that they also implement set operations that are faster than the same operation on a list.

Chapter 9

Real World Uses

This section contains some generator examples that illustrate some of the concepts mentioned previously.

9.1 Database chunking

The function fetch_many_wrapper was used in a business intelligence application to speed up fetching large datasets used for reporting. Because the datasets were potentially larger than the system memory, it was not possible to fetch the whole result at once. On the other hand, fetching each row incurred a large overhead due to latency for retrieving an item from the database. By fetching many items at once, this latency cost is amortized over many rows:

```
def fetch_many_wrapper(cursor, count=20000):
    """
    In an effort to speed up queries, this wrapper
    fetches count objects at a time. Otherwise our
    implementation has sqlalchemy fetching 1 row
    at a time (~30% slower).
    """
    done = False
    while not done:
        items = cursor.fetchmany(count)
        done = len(items) == 0
        if not done:
            for item in items:
                yield item
```

This generator fetches many items at once into a buffer, items. It then generates over the buffer. When items is empty, there is an attempt to fill up the buffer again. If the buffer is still empty, then fetching data from the database is done. By simply wrapping the loop over the database cursor with this generator improved performance by 30%.

9.2 Recursive generators

Generators that call themselves should *iterate over the recursive call*. This is different from a recursive function accumulating data into a list.

Here is a recursive function accumulating files in a directory:

```
def list_files(base_dir, recurse=True):
    results = []
    for name in os.listdir(base_dir):
        filepath = os.path.join(base_dir, name)
        if os.path.isdir(filepath) and recurse:
            results.extend(list_files(filepath, recurse))
        else:
            results.append(filepath)
    return results
```

Here is the conversion of the previous function into a generating version:

```
def find_files(base_dir, recurse=True):
    """
    yield files found in base_dir
    """
    for name in os.listdir(base_dir):
        filepath = os.path.join(base_dir, name)
        if os.path.isdir(filepath) and recurse:
            # make sure to iterate when recursing!
            for child in find_files(filepath, recurse):
                yield child
        else:
            yield filepath
```

Note that in the generating version the recursive call is iterated over, while in the accumulating version the results list is extended with the results of the recursive call.

Note that the above implementation is a simpler implementation of os.walk found in the standard library. os.walk also contains a similar recursive call:

```
def walk(top, topdown=True, onerror=None,
    followlinks=False):
    """Directory tree generator.

    For each directory in the directory tree rooted
    at top (including top itself, but excluding '.'
    and '..'), yields a 3-tuple

        dirpath, dirnames, filenames
    """

    islink, join, isdir = path.islink, path.join, \
                          path.isdir

    # We may not have read permission for top, in
    # which case we can't get a list of the files
    # the directory contains.  os.path.walk always
    # suppressed the exception then, rather than
    # blow up for a minor reason when (say) a
    #thousand readable directories are still
    # left to visit.  That logic is copied here.
    try:
        # Note that listdir and error are globals
        # in this module due to earlier import-*.
        names = listdir(top)
    except error, err:
        if onerror is not None:
            onerror(err)
        return

    dirs, nondirs = [], []
    for name in names:
        if isdir(join(top, name)):
            dirs.append(name)
        else:
            nondirs.append(name)

    if topdown:
        yield top, dirs, nondirs
    for name in dirs:
        new_path = join(top, name)
        if followlinks or not islink(new_path):
            for x in walk(new_path, topdown,
                          onerror, followlinks):
                yield x
```

```
if not topdown:
    yield top, dirs, nondirs
```

9.3   Examples from text tweaking

I created a program to aid me in converting a text dump from pdf to reStructuredText. What follows are more examples of processing that needed to be applied to various pdfs.

A *peeker* is a useful construct for determining when to continue iterating over a sequence. Rather than only have access to the result of the next call, a peeker will let you access an arbitrary number of items from the sequence. A peeker can look ahead during iteration. This is useful when it is necessary to look at multiple items to proceed to the next step, ie if you have three blank lines in a row from a text remove the last two.

Here is my peeker implementation:

```
class PeekDone(Exception):
    pass


class Peeker(object):
    def __init__(self, seq):
        self.seq = iter(seq)
        self.buffer = []

    def pop(self):
        if self.buffer:
            return self.buffer.pop(0)

    def peek(self, n=0):
        """ this can raise an exception if
        peeking off the end. Be aware and
        handle PeekDone appropriately
        """
        try:
            if n == len(self.buffer):
                self.buffer.append(self.seq.next())
        except StopIteration as e:
            raise PeekDone('Exhausted')
        return self.buffer[n]

    def __iter__(self):
        return self
```

```
def next(self):
    if self.buffer:
        return self.buffer.pop(0)
    else:
        return self.seq.next()
```

I use the PeekDone exception as a sentinel value, rather that returning a special value. Using the Peeker class can aid in processing text. Below is an example of a generator removing double blank lines from lines of text using Peeker:

```
def remove_double_returns(lines):
    lines = Peeker(lines)
    for line in lines:
        try:
            next_line = lines.peek()
        except PeekDone as e:
            yield line
            return

        if blank(next_line):
            yield line
            lines.pop()

        else:
            yield line
```

That could be done by someone fluent in awk in probably two lines. But here is one that appears to cross the line where a full fledged programming language makes the code more readable. It tries to remove multiple blank lines between paragraphs:

```
def fix_space_in_paragraph(lines):
    """ If paragraphs span pages (often) then
    there could be extra returns in the paragraphs....
    """
    lines = Peeker(lines)
    for line in lines:
        try:
            line2 = lines.peek()
        except PeekDone as e:
            yield line
            return
        try:
            line3 = lines.peek(1)
        except PeekDone as e:
```

```
            yield line
            yield line2
            return
    if blank(line2) and not ends_sentence(line):
        # don't use line2 so pop it
        lines.pop()
    yield line
```

Here is a simple generator without Peeker. It does the opposite of the previous lines and inserts an extra space between paragraphs. I need to ensure that paragraphs have an empty line between them so docutils does the right thing:

```
def insert_extra_paragraph_line(lines):
    for line in lines:
        if ends_paragraph(line):
            yield line
            yield '\n'
        else:
            yield line
```

In the end, using a chain of these generators, I was able to generate three mini-ebooks for my mother before she left for a week-long cruise.

My scripts for cleaning up the text looked something like this:

```
import sys

import ebookgen

def run():
    data = sys.stdin
    data = ebookgen.remove_leading_space(data)
    data = ebookgen.remove_dash_page(data)
    data = ebookgen.remove_carot_l(data)
    data = ebookgen.remove_two_spaces(data)
    data = ebookgen.remove_double_returns(data)
    data = ebookgen.insert_extra_paragraph_line(data)
    data = ebookgen.insert_rst_sections(data)
    for line in data:
        print line,

if __name__ == '__main__':
    run()
```

Part II

Decorators

Chapter 10

Functions

The basic definition of a function is simple in Python — it is a structure for abstracting a block of code that accepts input, does some processing, and returns output:

```
def function_name(input_1, input_2):
    # some processing
    return output
```

10.1 First-class functions

Unlike some languages, Python supports *first-class functions*. The idea that "functions [are] first-class citizens", coined in the 60's by British computer scientist Christopher Strachey, allows for functions to be passed into other functions, stored as variables and returned from functions. This is a hard requirement for functional languages such as Lisp. In Lisp, the function map takes a function as its first parameter and applies to members of the second parameter. Python also has a map function to perform an analogous operation. In contrast, the Java language does not support passing around functions.

10.2   Function instances

In Python, after a function is defined, the function name then refers to a function *instance*:

```
>>> def foo():
...     'docstring for foo'
...     print 'invoked foo'

>>> print foo
<function foo at 0x7f3916f02938>
```

Note that the above code did not *invoke* the function, it only printed out the string representation of the function foo.

Using the type function, the foo object can be introspected:

```
>>> type(foo)
<type 'function'>
```

In Python, there is a built-in class, function, for representing functions.

Also, functions can be assigned to other variables:

```
>>> bar = foo
>>> print bar
<function foo at 0x7f3916f02938>
```

Both foo and bar could be passed into other functions as arguments. They could also be returned as the result of invoking other functions:

```
>>> def get_foo():
...     return foo

>>> print get_foo
<function get_foo at 0x7ffe7c4408c0>
>>> print get_foo()
<function foo at 0x7f3916f02938>
```

Because functions can return other functions, it is possible to create function factories.

10.3   Invoking functions

This might seem obvious, but it bears mentioning here. Functions are *callable*. Because they are callable, they can be invoked. Python provides a way to introspect whether objects are invokable with the `callable` function:

```
>>> callable(foo)
True
```

> **Note**
>
> Python 3 removed the `callable` function. Two alternatives (that also work in Python 2.6 and above) are:
>
> ```
> >>> hasattr(foo, '__call__')
> ```
>
> and:
>
> ```
> >>> isinstance(foo, collections.Callable)
> ```

The invocation construct in Python is to add parentheses around any arguments to a callable object. To invoke `foo`, simply add parentheses (with no arguments since it has none) to it:

```
>>> foo()
invoked foo
```

> **Note**
>
> On a somewhat related note, if a class implements the `__call__` method, you can invoke instances of the class:
>
> ```
> >>> class CallMe:
> ...     def __call__(self):
> ...         print "Called"
> >>> c = CallMe()
> >>> c()
> Called
> ```
>
> This is subtle but this feature allows for using instances as decorators (or anything that is `callable` for that matter).

> **Note (cont.)**
>
> Note that functions also have __call__ methods, that
> are invoked under the hood as well.

10.4 Functions have attributes

Instances of classes in Python have attributes. Functions, being instances of function, likewise have attributes. Invoking
dir on the function instance will list the attributes:

```
>>> dir(foo)
['__call__', '__class__', '__closure__',
...
'__doc__',
...
'__name__',
'func_closure', 'func_code', 'func_defaults',
'func_dict', 'func_doc', 'func_globals', 'func_name']
```

As mentioned in the previous section, because functions
are *callable*, they have a __call__ method. Two other interesting attributes of functions are the func_name attribute and the
func_doc attribute, which have alternative *dunder* spellings
as well, __name__ and __doc__ respectively. Because the func_*
attributes are removed in Python 3 it is preferable to use the
dunder versions as they work in both Python 2 and 3:

```
>>> foo.__name__
'foo'
```

> **Note**
>
> Some Pythonistas have taken to calling methods that
> begin and end with double underscores "dunder" meth-
> ods.

A variable holding a function will also list the function's
name when asked, not the variable name:

```
>>> bar = foo
>>> bar.__name__
```

10.4. Functions have attributes

```
'foo'
```

The attribute ‗‗doc‗‗ is the *docstring* for the function:

```
>>> foo.__doc__
'docstring for foo'
```

> **Note**
>
> PEP 232, introduced *Function Attributes* in Python
> 2.1. Function attributes allow getting and setting of
> arbitrary members to function instances. This data is
> stored in the ‗‗dict‗‗ dictionary:
>
> ```
> >>> foo.note = 'more info'
> >>> foo.__dict__
> {'note': 'more info'}
> ```
>
> Note that ‗‗dict‗‗ is available in both Python 2 and
> 3.

> **Tip**
>
> Another function attribute is func‗defaults. Python
> stores default parameters in func‗defaults. It is sug-
> gested that default parameters use only non-mutable
> types. However, it is not uncommon to see Python be-
> ginners use [] as a default parameter. This eventually
> leads them down a debugging rabbit hole. To under-
> stand why, it is important to understand *when* the de-
> fault parameters are created. Default parameters are
> initialized during function definition time, which occurs
> at either module load time or during program execution.
> During module load time, globally defined functions
> are created. Because Python has first-class functions,
> functions can also be created and returned from inside
> the body of other function during runtime. When the
> function is created, the default parameters are examined
> and stored in the func‗defaults attribute.

65

Tip (cont.)

The following is a function that returns positive values from an iterable, but will also append them to another list, seq, if seq is passed into the function:

```
>>> def positive(items, seq=[]):
...     for item in items:
...         if item >= 0:
...             seq.append(item)
...     return seq
>>> positive
<function positive at 0x7ffe7c440b18>
>>> positive.func_defaults
([],)
```

In this case, the first and only item in func_defaults is an empty list, which is mutable. On the first invocation of positive, it appears to behave correctly:

```
>>> positive([1])
[1]
```

At this point, examining the func_defaults no longer shows that the default for seq should be an empty list. The list, being a mutable type, is still the same instance defined during function creation, but it is now populated from the interaction of the previous invocation:

```
>>> positive.func_defaults
([1],)
```

This leads to errors on subsequent invocations:

```
>>> positive([-2])
[1]
>>> positive([5])
[1, 5]

>>> positive.func_defaults
([1, 5],)
```

The general solution to resolve the need for mutable default parameters is to shift their creation from *module*

Tip (cont.)

import time to *runtime*. A common idiom is to have the parameter default to None then check for that value in the body of the function:

```
>>> def positive2(items, seq=None):
...     seq = seq or []
...     for item in items:
...         if item >= 0:
...             seq.append(item)
...     return seq

>>> positive2([1])
[1]
>>> positive2([-2])
[]
>>> positive2([5])
[5]
```

The above example was somewhat contrived to illustrate the problems with using mutable types as default parameters. If a function was needed to actually perform the logic of positive2, a more pythonic solution would be to use a list comprehension:

```
>>> items = [3, 4, -5]
>>> pos = seq.extend([x for x in items if x >= 0])
```

Note

The function attribute func_defaults becomes __defaults__ in Python 3. Note that unlike the other attributes that have extra dunder spellings in Python 2, __defaults__ does not exist in Python 2.

10.5 Function scope

Functions are defined in a *scope*. Within the body of a function, you can access the function itself, as well as anything that was in scope during the definition of the function. This enables *recursion* (a function being able to call itself), but also allows for reading and setting the attributes of a function while it is executing:

```
>>> def foo2():
...        print "NAME", foo2.__name__

>>> foo2()
NAME foo2
```

Any variable instances created within a function but not returned from it are *local* to the function and will be garbage collected when the function exits:

```
>>> def multiply(num1, num2):
...        result = 0
...        for i in range(num2):
...             result = result + num1
...        return result

>>> multiply(2, 10)
20
>>> print i
Traceback (most recent call last):
  File "<stdin>", line 1, in <module>
NameError: name 'i' is not defined
```

Given that the function name is in *global* scope within the body of that function, it is possible to attach data to the function while the the function is executing. It is also possible to attach data to a function outside of the function, even before it is ever executed:

```
>>> def foo3():
...        print foo3.stuff

>>> foo3.stuff = "Hello"

>>> foo3()
Hello
```

> **Note**
>
> The built-in functions locals and globals will return a mapping of names to objects that their respective namespaces contain:

Note (cont.)

```
>>> def local_test():
...      a = 1
...      b = 'b'
...      print locals()

>>> local_test()
{'a': 1, 'b': 'b'}

>>> globals()
{'bar': <function foo at 0x840b90>,
 '__builtins__': {'bytearray': <type 'bytearray'>,
  ...
  'foo': <function foo at 0x840b90>,
  'foo3': <function foo3 at 0x9372a8>}
```

10.6   Functions can be nested

Another feature that falls out of this notion of first-class functions is the ability to *nest* functions. In addition to just returning a function as a result of an invocation, a function can be
defined within another function and then returned:

```
>>> def adder():
...      def add(x, y):
...            return x + y
...      return add

>>> adder()
<function add at 0x7ffe7c440a28>
>>> adder()(2, 4)
6
```

Note

If the above example were in a Python program, the
adder function would be created at module import time.
The inner function, add, on the other hand, does not
exist when the module is imported. It is created during
runtime, when the adder function is invoked. Every

> **Note (cont.)**
>
> invocation of adder will create a new instance of add as illustrated by their changing id below:
>
> ```
> >>> adder()
> <function add at 0x7ffe7c440aa0>
> >>> adder()
> <function add at 0x7ffe7c440a28>
> ```

Nested functions in Python also create the need for nested scope. Any nested function has read/write access to built-ins and globals. Also nested functions have read-only access to variables defined in the enclosing functions:

```
>>> x = 5 # "global" variable
>>> y = 3
>>> def wrapper():
...     def inner():
...         # can't write x unless
...         # global is used ie
...         # UnboundLocalError
...         global x
...         x = 6
...         y = -2 # now local shadows global
...         # z is a "free" variable in inner
...         print "Inner", x, y, z
...     y = 1 # now local
...     z = 0
...     inner()
...     print "Wrap", x, y, z

>>> wrapper()
Inner 6 -2 0
Wrap 6 1 0
>>> print "Global", x, y
Global 6 3
```

In the previous example, x and y are global variables. Within wrapper, read-only access is available for the global x. Inside of the inner function, x is marked with the global keyword, which marks the x as a reference to the global x. In both functions, wrapper and inner, y *shadows* the global y. At any point inside a function when a variable is defined, it becomes *local*, unless it was previously marked with the `global` keyword.

A *free variable*, is a computer science term for a variable that is neither local nor passed in as a argument to a function. Within the function `inner`, z is a free variable. In Python terms, a variable defined in an enclosing function is a free variable inside any nested functions.

> **Note**
>
> Though there can be multiple nested scopes within arbitrarily nested functions, only the global scope is writeable.

> **Note**
>
> Python 3 introduced the `nonlocal` keywords which allows for finer grained modification of non-global variables:

```
>>> # running in Python 3
>>> def wrapper():
...     b = 8
...     def inner():
...         print('1', b)
...         nonlocal b
...         b = 10
...     print('2', b)
...     inner()
...     print('3', b)

>>> wrapper()
1 8
2 8
3 10
```

Chapter 11

Function Parameters

Python supports four different types of parameters for functions.

- Normal Parameters - Have a name and a position

- Keyword (default/named) Paramenters - Have a name

- Variable Parameters - Preceded by an *, have a position

- Variable Keyword Parameters - Preceded by a **, have a name

11.1   Parameters vs arguments

For computer science pedants, there is a slight distinction in the definition of *parameters* and *arguments*. Parameters are the names of variables accepted for input in the definition of a function. Arguments are the variables passed into an invoked function:

```
>>> def mult(a, b):
...     return a * b

>>> x = 3
>>> y = 2
>>> print mult(x, y)
6
```

In the above code, a and b are *parameters* because they appear in the definition of the function. x and y are *arguments*.

This is a slight distinction in Python, and it is pretty common to see them used interchangeably. In fact the common naming scheme for variable parameters is `*args` and variable keyword parameters is `**kwargs`.

11.2 Normal and keyword parameters

Normal and keyword parameters are very common. Most Python developers run into the mutable default parameter gotcha at some point. The only real difference between these two parameter types is that normal parameters are always required in functions declaring them. Like keyword parameters, normal parameters also support using the `name=value` argument style during invocation:

```
>>> def normal(a, b, c):
...     print a, b, c


>>> normal(1, 2, 3)
1 2 3

>>> normal(a=1, b=2, c=3)
1 2 3
```

If the arguments have their name provided during invocation, then the order of the parameters is not important:

```
>>> normal(c=3, a=1, b=2)
1 2 3
```

11.3 Variable parameters

In addition to serving as the multiplication and power operators — the asterisk, *, denotes *variable parameters* in function and method definitions. Variable parameters allow a function to take an arbitrary number of position based arguments. For example in the C world, the `printf` function, allows for any number of arguments to be passed into it. A simple example in Python follows:

```
>>> def printf(fmt, *args):
...     done = False
...     start = 0
...     tup_idx = 0
...     while not done:
...         i = fmt.find('%s', start)
...         if i == -1:
...             done = True
...         else:
...             word = str(args[tup_idx])
...             tup_idx = tup_idx + 1
...             fmt = fmt[:i] + word + fmt[i+2:]
...             start = i + 1 + len(word)
...     print fmt

>>> printf('hello')
hello
>>> printf('My name: %s', 'Matt')
My name: Matt
>>> printf('nums: %s, %s, %s', *range(1, 4))
nums: 1, 2, 3
```

> **Note**
>
> Variable parameters are commonly labeled as *args.
> Much like self is the accepted Python naming conven-
> tion for the first parameter to a method for an object,
> *args is the standard naming convention used for vari-
> able parameters. In reality, the Python interpreter does
> not care what the name of the parameter following the
> asterisk is. Because there can only be one parameter de-
> fined as a variable parameter (not including the variable
> *keyword* parameter), it is common convention to spell
> the variable parameter as *args.

By prefixing a parameter with an *, like *args, the function will allow any number of arguments for that parameter
(including 0 arguments). Within the function itself, the variable args (without an *) will be a tuple containing all the
arguments passed into the function:

```
>>> def demo_args(*args):
...     print type(args), args
```

```
>>> demo_args()
<type 'tuple'> ()
>>> demo_args(1)
<type 'tuple'> (1,)
>>> demo_args(3, 'foo')
<type 'tuple'> (3, 'foo')
```

> **Note**
>
> Variable parameters are commonly combined with variable keyword parameters. Together they are seen in the constructors of subclasses. This allows a subclass to easily accept any of the arguments for a parent class without enumerating any of them.
>
> Variable parameters and variable keyword parameters are also used for decorators which are described later in this book.

11.4 The * operator

The asterisk serves to:

- apply multiplication (4*2)

- apply the power operator (4**2)

- mark variable parameters

- flatten argument sequences, the *splat* operator

- mark variable keyword parameters

- flatten keywords dictionaries, the *splat* operator

The last two will be discussed later in the following sections. The previous section discussed variable parameters. Flattening arguments is next in the list. What if you already have appropriate arguments for a function sitting around in a sequence? Is it necessary to pull each item out during function invocation?

```
>>> vars = ['John', 'Paul']
>>> demo_args(vars[0], vars[1])
<type 'tuple'> ('John', 'Paul')
```

The * operator is also overloaded to *flatten* a sequence of arguments during invocation of a function. Some refer to this as *splatting* a sequence. The following is equivalent to the previous line:

```
>>> demo_args(*vars)
<type 'tuple'> ('John', 'Paul')
```

If the * is left off the vars argument, args would be tuple containing a single item, the list with the two parameters. This is probably not what was intended if vars was meant to contain the parameters for a function:

```
>>> demo_args(vars)
<type 'tuple'> (['John', 'Paul'],)
```

In the definition of demo_args, the args parameter will accept any number of arguments. Within the body of demo_args, args is a tuple holding those values. In the previous case, a single argument containing a list was passed into the function, therefore, args within the function will be a tuple with only one item, the list that was passed in.

Tip

When invoking functions declared with variable arguments, make sure you understand which arguments need to be flattened. (Usually for decorators and constructors they should all be flattened).

It also is possible to flatten a sequence of arguments into a function that does not have any variable parameters:

```
>>> def add3(a, b, c):
...     return a + b + c

>>> add3(*[4, 5, 6])
15
```

> **Note**
>
> Only a single sequence may be flattened into a function:

```
>>> demo_args(*vars, *vars)
Traceback (most recent call last):
  ...
    demo_args(*vars, *vars)
                      ^
SyntaxError: invalid syntax
```

> **Note**
>
> If a function has normal, keyword and variable parameters, it may be invoked with just a flattened sequence. In that case the sequence will populate the normal and keyword parameters, and any left over variables will be left in the variable argument:

```
>>> def func(a, b='b', *args):
...     print [x for x in [a, b, args]]

>>> vars = (3, 4, 5)
>>> func(*vars)
[3, 4, (5,)]
```

> Again, because the * *flattens* the arguments, they fill out the parameters. The above invocation is the same as calling the function with the arguments listed out:

```
>>> func(vars[0], vars[1], vars[2])
[3, 4, (5,)]
```

11.5   Variable keyword parameters

Similar to variable parameters, Python also allows *variable keyword parameters*. Using the ** syntax, a parameter can be marked to allow any number of keyword arguments:

```
>>> def demo_kwargs(**kwargs):
...     print type(kwargs), kwargs
```

```
>>> demo_kwargs()
<type 'dict'> {}

>>> demo_kwargs(one=1)
<type 'dict'> {'one': 1}

>>> demo_kwargs(one=1, two=2)
<type 'dict'> {'two': 2, 'one': 1}
```

The **, when used within a function or method definition, indicates that a function will take any number of keyword arguments. The arguments arrive in a dictionary containing the names and their corresponding values. Similar to args, kwargs is the standard convention for a parameter name used for variable keyword parameters.

> **Note**
>
> Variable keyword parameters require arguments to provide a name:
>
> ```
> >>> demo_kwargs(1)
> Traceback (most recent call last):
>   ...
>     demo_kwargs(1)
> TypeError: demo_kwargs() takes exactly 0
> arguments (1 given)
> ```
>
> This error can be a little confusing, since demo_kwargs takes zero *normal* parameters, but any number of *keyword* parameters.

11.6 Flattening dictionaries

The double asterisks also serves to *flatten* — or *splat* — a dictionary into keyword arguments for a function:

```
>>> def distance(x1, y1, x2, y2):
...     return ((x1-x2)**2 +
...             (y1-y2)**2) ** .5

>>> points = {'x1':1, 'y1':1,
...           'x2':4, 'y2':5}
```

```
>>> distance(**points)
5.0
```

The above invocation of distance is the same as calling the function with the items of the dictionary listed as keyword arguments:

```
>>> distance(x1=1, y1=1, x2=4, y2=5)
5.0
```

Dictionaries can also be flattened into functions with just normal parameters — such as distance or functions defined to take variable keyword parameters — such as demo_kwargs:

```
>>> demo_kwargs(**points)
<type 'dict'> {'y1': 1, 'x2': 4,
'x1': 1, 'y2': 5}
```

11.7 Arbitrary function parameters

A function that has both variable parameters and variable keyword parameters can take an arbitrary number of arguments, be they passed in as normal, keyword, or variable arguments. This makes using the combination of them prime candidates for the parameters of subclass constructors and decorators.

Here are the four types of parameters:

- normal

- keyword

- variable

- variable keyword

Here is a function that has all four types of parameters:

```
>>> def demo_params(normal, kw="Test", *args, **kwargs):
...     print normal, kw, args, kwargs
```

Tip

Functions may only define one variable parameter
and one variable keyword parameter. Also, the order
of the parameter definition must follow the order of the
four types of parameters listed above.

Tip

Remember when invoking functions with the splat
operator — with either variable arguments or variable
keyword arguments — it is the same as if those arguments are listed out individually. If variable keyword
arguments keys have the same name as normal or keyword parameters, they can be used for them. Other-
wise, variable arguments would come after the normal
and keyword arguments, and variable keyword arguments would appear after that with their corresponding
names:

```
>>> args = (0, 1, 2)
>>> kw = {'foo': 3, 'bar': 4}

>>> demo_params(*args, **kw)
0 1 (2,) {'foo': 3, 'bar': 4}
```

Notice that the variable parameters flowed into the
normal and keyword parameters. Again, this invocation
is equivalent to:

```
>>> demo_params(args[0], args[1], args[2],
...             foo=3, bar=4)
0 1 (2,) {'foo': 3, 'bar': 4}
```

Chapter 12

Closures

Closures have an aura around them that makes them appear unapproachable. It does not help that the descriptions of them are terse:

> [A] *closure* (also lexical closure, function closure, function value or functional value) is a function together with a referencing environment for the non-local variables of that function. A closure allows a function to access variables outside its typical scope. Such a function is said to be "closed over" its *free variables*.

> Wikipedia

A closure in Python is simply a function that is returned by another function:

```
>>> def add_x(x):
...     def adder(num):
...         # adder is a closure
...         # x is a free variable
...         return x + num
...     return adder

>>> add_5 = add_x(5)
>>> add_5
<function adder at ...>
>>> add_5(10)
15
```

In the above example, the function add_x returns an inner function. The inner function, adder, is "closed over" — hence a *closure*. Inside of adder, the variable x is a *free variable* because it is non-local to adder and defined outside of it. A simplified definition of a Python closure might be:

> In Python functions can return new functions. The inner function is a *closure* and any variable it accesses that are defined outside of that function are *free variables*.

12.1 Common uses of closures

As illustrated in the previous section, closures are useful as function factories. Here are some other uses:

- To keep a common interface (the *adapter pattern*)

- To eliminate code duplication

- To delay execution of a function

A real-life example is creating a filter for tabular results:

```
>>> def db_results(query_filter, table):
...     results = []
...     for row in table:
...         result = query_filter(row)
...         if result:
...             results.append(result)
...     return results
```

Where a query_filter takes the form:

```
>>> def query_filter(row):
...     # filter row of table
...     return filtered_row or None
```

Assuming that tables are composed of lists of dictionaries, a filter for name might look like this:

```
>>> def matt_filter(row):
...     if row['name'].lower() == 'matt':
...         return row
```

```
>>> matt_filter({'name':'Matt'})
{'name': 'Matt'}

>>> matt_filter({'name':'Fred'}) is None
True
```

But as often occurs, filtering by other names might be required as well. A closure can be used to easily create different name filters:

```
>>> def name_filter(name):
...     def inner(row):
...         if row['name'].lower() == name.lower():
...             return row
...     return inner

>>> paul_filter = name_filter('Paul')
>>> john_filter = name_filter('John')
>>> george_filter = name_filter('George')
>>> ringo_filter = name_filter('Ringo')
```

Closures also enable filtering by multiple filters. An *or* operation that takes multiple filters can be created using a closure as well:

```
>>> def or_op(filters):
...     def inner(row):
...         for f in filters:
...             if f(row):
...                 return row
...     return inner

>>> beatle = or_op([paul_filter,
...     john_filter,
...     ringo_filter,
...     george_filter])

>>> beatle({'name':'Matt'}) is None
True
>>> beatle({'name':'John'})
{'name': 'John'}
```

These simple functions illustrate the power of closures. Closures quickly enable generation of functions and conforming to a interface (the adapter pattern).

Chapter 13

Decorators

According to Wikipedia, a decorator is "a design pattern that allows behavior to be added to an existing object dynamically". In Python, a decorator is a method for altering a callable. Closures enable the creation of decorators. A decorated callable can be altered at the following times:

- before invocation

- during invocation — the implementation can be changed/replaced

- after invocation

Normally the callables that are decorated in Python are either functions or methods.

13.1 A simple decorator

Here is a decorator, verbose, that prints out the name of the function it decorates before and after execution:

```
>>> def verbose(func):
...     def wrapper():
...         print "Before", func.__name__
...         result = func()
...         print "After", func.__name__
...         return result
...     return wrapper
```

Please make sure you understand what the verbose function does. It accepts a function, func, and returns a new function, wrapper. When wrapper is invoked, it will print the name, execute the original wrapped function, print the name again and return the result of the original function. This is about as simple as a decorator can get, and the others that follow will build upon this same pattern.

A decorator is really only useful when applied to a function. There are two ways to do this. The first is to simply invoke the decorator on a function:

```
>>> def hello():
...      print "Hello"

>>> hello = verbose(hello)
```

The above redefines the function hello, as the function returned by verbose. Examining the __name__ attribute shows that the new function is actually wrapper:

```
>>> hello.__name__
'wrapper'
```

Now, when hello is invoked, it prints a message before and after executing:

```
>>> hello()
Before hello
Hello
After hello
```

As described in PEP 318, Python 2.4 provided the second method of wrapping a function. The syntactic sugar to decorate a function is illustrated below:

```
>>> @verbose
... def greet():
...      print "G'day"
```

Placing @verbose immediately before the function definition is the same as writing greet = verbose(greet) following the function:

```
>>> greet()
Before greet
G'day
```

```
After greet
```

Tip

The PEP 318 style of decorating does not require parentheses following verbose. It will result in an error if attempted:

```
>>> @verbose()
... def howdy()
...     print "Howdy"
Traceback (most recent call last):
    ...
    def howdy()
              ^
SyntaxError: invalid syntax
```

The verbose decorator actually has an issue. It only works with functions that do not have parameters:

```
>>> @verbose
... def add(x, y):
...     return x + y

>>> add(2, 3)
Traceback (most recent call last):
    ...
    add(2, 3)
TypeError: wrapper() takes no arguments (2 given)
```

As mentioned in the error, wrapper takes no arguments. The closure, wrapper, was defined without parameters. Because wrapper is invoked under the covers when add is invoked, the error is raised. The solution is simple — add parameters. But how many parameters? The function add takes two, but hello and greet take none. The answer is to use *variable parameters*. As mentioned in the variable parameters section, using these types of parameters enables a function to accept an arbitrary number of arguments:

```
>>> def chatty(func):
...     def wrapper(*args, **kwargs):
...         print "Before", func.__name__
...         result = func(*args, **kwargs)
```

```
...            print "After", func.__name__
...            return result
...      return wrapper

>>> @chatty
... def mult(x, y):
...      return x * y

>>> mult(2, 4)
Before mult
After mult
8


>>> @chatty
... def goodbye():
...      print "Later"

>>> goodbye()
Before goodbye
Later
After goodbye
```

13.2   A decorator template

What follows is a template for a decorator. This template
accepts functions that take an arbitrary amount of arguments:

```
>>> def decorator(func_to_decorate):
...      def wrapper(*args, **kwargs):
...          # do something before invocation
...          result = func_to_decorate(*args, **kwargs)
...          # do something after
...          return result
...      wrapper.__doc__ = func_to_decorate.__doc__
...      wrapper.__name__ = func_to_decorate.__doc__
...      return wrapper
```

There are two lines in this template that were not present
in the previous examples. In well-behaved decorators the
__doc__ and __name__ of the wrapper function need to be updated with the values from the function that is being decorated. For *pickling* (serialization to disk) of objects, it is
required that __name__ is updated. The __doc__ attribute is
updated so the function is friendly to introspection.

Note

The function wraps (which is a decorator itself) found in the functools module, will update __doc__ and __name__ as well. So another template is:

```
>>> import functools

>>> def decorator(func_to_decorate):
...     @functools.wraps(func_to_decorate)
...     def wrapper(*args, **kwargs):
...         # do something before invocation
...         result = func_to_decorate(*args,
...                                        **kwargs)
...         # do something after
...         return result
...     return wrapper
```

The __module__ attribute is also updated by wraps.

Note

As was discussed in the closure section, any *callable* can wrap another function. So a callable can also serve as a decorator. Here is an example of a class that can be used to decorate functions:

```
>>> class decorator_class(object):
...     def __init__(self, function):
...         self.function = function
...     def __call__(self, *args, **kwargs):
...         # do something before invocation
...         result = self.function(*args,
...                                    **kwargs)
...         # do something after
...         return result
```

This class decorator could be used as follows:

```
>>> @decorator_class
... def function():
...     # implementation
```

> **Note**
>
> The above decorator is not the same as what is known as a *Class Decorator* in Python. These are discussed in PEP 3129.

13.3 Parameterized decorators

Often a decorator needs to be customized on a per function basis. For example the Django `require_http_methods` decorator decorates a view and ensures that it uses the correct http methods — GET, HEAD, POST, PUT, etc — or a combination of those methods. This decorator is a *parameterized* decorator that can be customized for the specific function it is wrapping. To enforce GET on a view, wrapping with `@require_http_methods(["GET"])` is sufficient. If a different function required GET or POST, `@require_http_methods(["GET", "POST"])` customizes the behavior for that function. How does this work, when it was mentioned previously that a decorator will throw an error if it uses parentheses when wrapping a function?

Previous chapters have discussed how to implement a function factory in Python. How is it done? The usual manner is — use a *closure* to generate a new function. Hence *the method to generate a parameterizable decorator is to wrap the decorator with another function*! The parameterized decorator itself is actually a decorator generator.

Make sure you understand the previous paragraph because it tends to cause people's heads to hurt until they understand what is going on.

If business logic required truncating results from functions to a certain length — 5, a single generator could do that. Any function that possibly generated results longer than 5 could be decorated to limit the length of the results:

```
>>> def trunc(func):
...     def wrapper(*args, **kwargs):
...         result = func(*args, **kwargs)
...         return result[:5]
...     return wrapper
```

```
>>> @trunc
... def data():
...     return "foobar"

>>> data()
'fooba'
```

Now assume that the requirement for truncation is changed. One function must be truncated to a length of 3 while another function might need to have a length of 6. What follows is a simple parameterized decorator — or a function that generates customized decorators — that limits the length of the result of the decorated function:

```
>>> def limit(length):
...     def decorator(func):
...         def wrapper(*args, **kwargs):
...             result = func(*args, **kwargs)
...             return result[:length]
...         return wrapper
...     return decorator

>>> @limit(3)
... def data3():
...     return "limit to 3"


>>> data3()
'lim'

>>> @limit(6)
... def data6():
...     return "limit to 6"

>>> data6()
'limit '
```

> **Note**
>
> The syntactic sugar for decorating with parameterized decorators is to declare the decorator before the function definition:
>
> ```
> >>> @limit(3)
> ... def data3():
> ```

Note (cont.)

```
...        return "limit to 3"
```

It is the same as the following:

```
>>> def data3():
...        return "limit to 3"
>>> data3 = limit(3)(data3)
```

When the function limit is invoked (with 3 as its parameter), it returns (or generates) a function — a decorator. This decorator, aptly named decorator, is then invoked with the function to decorate, data3.

13.4   Parameterized template

A template for a parameterized decorator follows:

```
>>> def param_dec(option):
...        def decorator(function):
...            def wrapper(*args, **kwargs):
...                # probably use option in here
...                # before
...                result = function(*args, **kwargs)
...                # after
...                return result
...            wrapper.__doc__ = function.__doc__
...            wrapper.__name__ = function.__name__
...            return wrapper
...        return decorator
```

13.5   Multiple decorators

Just as functions can be nested arbitrarily inside of other functions, functions can be wrapped by multiple decorators:

```
>>> @chatty
... @limit(2)
... def greet():
...        return 'Greetings'

>>> print greet()
Before wrapper
```

```
After wrapper
Gr
```

The decorating syntactic sugar is the same as:

```
>>> greet = chatty(limit(2)(greet))
```

Another way to think of these nested decorators is that the topmost decorator is the outermost decorator, and wraps the result of any inner decorator.

13.6 Common uses for decorators

Remember that decorators can alter or inspect the:

- function arguments
- function being wrapped
- results of the function

With that in mind there are common instances where decorators are used.

- Caching expensive calculations
- Retrying a function that might fail
- Redirecting `sys.stdout` to capture what a function prints to it
- Logging the amount of time spent in a function
- Timing out a function call
- Access control

Chapter 14

Alternate Decorator Implementations

Most decorators are implemented by functions or classes. But a decorator broken down to its most basic form is *a callable that returns a callable.* As such decorators can be implemented in various ways. Here are a few examples of the *identity decorator* implemented using different methods. This decorator simply returns the function that is decorated. It is not particularly useful, but is interesting to illustrate a few properties of decorators.

The first decorator example is a lambda function that returns the function passed into it. In practice this decorator will not be able to modify input or output, but for the identity decorator it does the job:

```
>>> iden1 = lambda func: func
```

The second example is a lambda function that returns another lambda function. This has limited support for modifying input and output:

```
>>> iden2 = lambda func: lambda *args, **kwargs: \
...     func(*args, **kwargs)
```

This example illustrates the failures of trying to do too much in a lambda function. It tries to combine a wrapper function inside of a lambda statement. Because lambdas only support an *expression* in their body (a function is a *compound statement*), Python actually throws a SyntaxError when trying to parse it:

```
>>> iden3 = lambda func: \
...     def wrapper(*args, **kwargs):
...         func(*args, **kwargs)
Traceback (most recent call last):
  ...
    def wrapper(*args, **kwargs):
      ^
SyntaxError: invalid syntax
```

This fourth example is probably the simplest—a function that returns the function passed to it:

```
>>> def iden4(func):
...     return func
```

This next decorator is the opposite of the attempt in iden3, use a lambda function as the wrapper function. It does the job for the identity decorator, but again suffers from the limited functionality available in a lambda body—only expressions.

```
>>> def iden5(func):
...     return lambda *args, **kwargs: func(
...         *args, **kwargs)
```

The decorator below is the canonical decorator template, dressed up to serve as the identity decorator:

```
>>> def iden6(func):
...     @functools.wraps(func)
...     def wrapper(*args, **kwargs):
...         return func(*args, **kwargs)
...     return wrapper
```

Below is the canonical class that serves as a decorator. I prefer to violate PEP 8 naming conventions here because the use is similar to function decorators:

```
>>> class iden7(object):
...     def __init__(self, func):
...         self.func = func
...     def __call__(self, *args, **kwargs):
...         return self.func(*args, **kwargs)
```

While all of the previous decorators can wrap functions using the explicit wrapping syntax (found in Python versions prior to 2.4), the lambda decorators will not work with the PEP 318 syntactic sugar in a doctest. This is strange behaviour, perhaps showing that the author should be wary of relying too heavily on doctest. Merely listing the lambda name following @ will raise a SyntaxError:

```
>>> @iden1
Traceback (most recent call last):
  ...
    @iden1
         ^
SyntaxError: unexpected EOF while parsing
```

But explicit wrapping works for lambda decorators in doctests:

```
>>> def add1(x, y):
...     return x + y

>>> add1 = iden1(add1)
>>> add1(2, 3)
5
```

Oddly enough the syntactic sugar also works from the interpreter.

The following two decorators are classes whose *instances* serve as decorators. Here the class naming does not conflict with PEP 8 conventions as the class name is used to create an instance rather than doing the actual decorating:

```
>>> class Iden8(object):
...     def __init__(self):
...         pass
...     def __call__(self, func):
...         return lambda *args, **kwargs: func(
...             *args, **kwargs)

>>> class Iden9(object):
...     def __init__(self):
```

```
...          pass
...      def __call__(self, func):
...          @functools.wraps(func)
...          def wrapper(*args, **kwargs):
...              return func(*args, **kwargs)
...          return wrapper

>>> class Iden10(object):
...      def __init__(self):
...          pass
...      def __call__(self, func):
...          dec = Iden(9)
...          return dec(func)
```

For these classes, an instance of them must be used to decorate:

```
>>> iden8 = Iden8()
>>> @iden8
>>> def add2(x, y):
...      return x + y

>>> add2(4, 5)
9
```

Note

One possible advantage of class instance decorators is that they could be modified at runtime. In the contrived example below, the decorator takes an argument to limit how long the result can be:

```
>>> class Limit(object):
...      def __init__(self, size):
...          self.size = size
...      def __call__(self, func):
...          @functools.wraps(func)
...          def wrapper(*args, **kwargs):
...              return func(*args,
...                  **kwargs)[:self.size]
...          return wrapper
```

Here an instance is created that limits to lengths of two and a function is decorated with said instance:

```
>>> limit = Limit(2)
```

One last example of a callable returning a callable is a function returning a partial:

```
>>> def iden11(func):
...      return functools.partial(func)

>>> @iden11
>>> def add11(x, y):
...      return x + y

>>> add11(3, 1)
4
```

14.1 Well behaved?

Well behaved decorators use either functool.wraps or up-date __name__, __doc__, and __module__ (needed for pickling and introspection). By this measure iden2, (or any lambda decorator that is not the identity decorator implemented as iden1) will not conform to this property:

```
>>> def sub(x, y):
...      '''subtraction'''
...      return x - y

>>> sub2 = iden2(sub)
```

```
>>> sub2.__name__  # should be iden2
'<lambda>'

>>> sub2.__doc__  # should be 'subtraction'
```

iden1 (and iden4) works here because it returns the original function, not one wrapped in another function or lambda statement. But it is not possible to update these properties in iden2.

The decorator iden5 (a lambda inside a function) fails this test as well. An improved version will remedy this:

```
>>> def iden5plus(func):
...     x = lambda *args, **kwargs: func(*args,
...         **kwargs)
...     x.__name__ = func.__name__
...     x.__doc__ = func.__doc__
...     x.__module__ = func.__module__
...     return x

>>> sub5 = iden5plus(sub)
>>> sub5.__name__
'sub'
```

The class decorator also fails here to update the proper attributes:

```
>>> sub7 = iden7(sub)
>>> sub7.__name__
Traceback (most recent call last):
  ...
AttributeError: 'iden7' object has no attribute
'__name__'
```

A tweaked version of the class decorator can deal with these issues in the constructor:

```
>>> class iden7plus(object):
...     def __init__(self, func):
...         self.func = func
...         self.__doc__ = func.__doc__
...         self.__name__ = func.__name__
...         self.__module__ = func.__module__
...     def __call__(self, *args, **kwargs):
...         return self.func(*args, **kwargs)

>>> sub7 = iden7plus(sub)
>>> sub7.__name__
```

```
'sub'
```

Iden8 would need its lambda modified in a similar style to iden5plus. Because Iden9 includes functools.wraps it is well behaved:

```
>>> iden9 = Iden9()
>>> sub9 = iden9(sub)
>>> sub9.__name__
'sub'
```

The partial decorator also fails this out of the box:

```
>>> sub11 = iden11(sub)
>>> sub11.__name__
Traceback (most recent call last):
  ...
AttributeError: 'functools.partial' object has no
attribute '__name__'
```

Here is an improved partial:

```
>>> def iden11plus(func):
...     new_func = functools.partial(func)
...     new_func.__name__ = func.__name__
...     new_func.__doc__ = func.__doc__
...     new_func.__module__ = func.__module__
...     return new_func

>>> sub11 = iden11plus(sub)
>>> sub11.__name__
'sub'
```

Even though different types of callables can serve to create decorators, not all of these types play well in practice. Lambda statements in particular should probably be shied away from due to the limited functionality they provide.

14.2   Decorating methods

So far the discussion has revolved around decorating callables that are functions. Often it is desirable to decorate methods. Naïvely, one would expect this to "just work":

```
>>> class Mult:
...     def __init__(self):
...         pass
```

```
...        def doit2(self, x, y):
...            return x * y
...        doit2 = iden2(doit2)
...
...        @iden6
...        def doit6(self, x, y):
...            return x * y
...
...        @iden7plus
...        def doit7(self, x, y):
...            return x * y
...
...        @iden9
...        def doit9(self, x, y):
...            return x * y
...
...        @iden11plus
...        def doit11(self, x, y):
...            return x * y
...        doit11 = iden11plus(doit11)
```

This should work for identity lambdas:

```
>>> mult = Mult()
>>> mult.doit2(2,3)
6
```

And decorators created with functions:

```
>>> mult.doit6(1,3)
3
```

What about decorators implemented as classes?

```
>>> mult.doit7(1,2)
Traceback (most recent call last):
  ...
TypeError: doit7() takes exactly 3 arguments (2 given)
```

Whoops! What is going on here? At the time of decoration, doit7 is an *unbound method*, a *bound method* is attached to an instance but there is no class instance to attach it to. When the method doit7 is invoked it is actually invoked on the instance not the unbound method. Using the descriptor protocol the decorator can be updated and bound to the instance. This is done by adding the following __get__ method to the decorator class:

```
>>> class iden7plusplus(object):
```

```
...       def __init__(self, func):
...           self.func = func
...           self.__doc__ = func.__doc__
...           self.__name__ = func.__name__
...           self.__module__ = func.__module__
...
...       def __call__(self, *args, **kwargs):
...           return self.func(*args, **kwargs)
...
...       def __get__(self, obj_self, objtype):
...           return functools.partial(self.__call__,
...             obj_self)
```

Here is a new class method using that decorator:

```
>>> class Mult2:
...       @iden7plusplus
...       def doit7(self, x, y):
...           return x * y

>>> mult2 = Mult2()
>>> mult2.doit7(1,2)
2
```

Because the class instance decorator does not actually store an instance to the unbound method, it works without any further hackery:

```
>>> mult.doit9(1,5)
5
```

Sadly, the partial decorator also falls victim to the unbound method problem. The author is not motivated to find a solution to this (attaching a __get__ method to the partial does not work) because function decorators "just work":

```
>>> mult.doit11(2,5)
Traceback (most recent call last):
  ...
TypeError: doit11() takes exactly 3 arguments (2 given)
```

There are issues with decorators implemented with non-functions, I recommend using functions for decorators. Below is a table summarizing the differences.

Decorator type	Doctest Sugar	Well-behaved	Works w/ unbound method
function	Y	Y	Y
lambda	N	N	Y
class	Y	Y	N
class instance	N	Y	Y
partial	N	Y	N

Note

If you really want to use classes to decorate—some claim they fit their brain better—here is a template for parameterized class decorators:

```
>>> class decorator:
...     def __init__(self, option):
...         self.option = option
...
...     def __call__(self, func):
...         @functools.wraps(func)
...         def wrapper(*args, **kwargs):
...             # do something with option
...             return func(*args, **kwargs)
...         return wrapper
```

Because the decorated function will be invoked when it is bound (in the __call__ method rather than __init__) there is no need to implement the descriptor protocol for __get__.

Part III

Functional Programming and Comprehension Constructs

Chapter 15

Functional Constructs in Python

Python functions are *first-class functions*. Languages that have first-class functions, treat functions as data. Like data, functions can be passed into other functions, or returned from other functions. Python has a built-in type—*function*—that is used to represent an instance of a function. The Java language, for example, does not have support for first-class functions (or methods). In Java, methods can only be invoked. Python in addition to allowing functions to be invoked, also allows for functions to be passed around—first-class functions.

A function exists in the namespace it is defined in. When a function name alone (not *invoked* with parentheses) is typed into the REPL, the interpreter notes that there is an instance defined in the global namespace:

```
>>> def simple():
...     print "invoked"

>>> simple  # note no parentheses
<function simple at 0x7f1c1f4ad9b0>
```

The function was not invoked above, the interpreter printed out a string representation of it. To invoke a function we need to call it by adding parentheses:

```
>>> simple()  # invocation
invoked
```

This function can be passed into another function that invokes it, illustrating that functions can serve as data:

```
>>> def call_twice(func):
...     func()
...     func()

>>> call_twice(simple)
invoked
invoked
```

First-class functions enable functional constructs in Python. These constructs were added to Python in version 1.4. They include `lambda`, `map`, `reduce` and `filter`. Programmers familiar with Lisp or Scheme will be familiar with these constructs.

Note

For the curious Guido has written on the Origins of Python's "Functional" Features. This blog post explains the history of `lambda` and how it came to be crippled*.

---

*http://python-history.blogspot.com/2009/04/origins-of-pythons-functional-features.html

Chapter 16

lambda

lambda functions offer a subset of the functionality of normal functions. However, they are important in functional programming, and worth understanding. Simple one-liner functions are prime candidates for lambda expressions. Because of the difference in the appearance between lambda and normal functions (ie parameter definitions lack parentheses), and terseness, some programmers (especially those without a functional programming background) find lambda functions harder to understand and frown upon their use.

The lambda expression is used to create one line anonymous functions in Python. Here is a statement that defines a function to multiply two numbers:

```
>>> mul = lambda x, y: x * y
```

This creates a function, mul, that accepts two arguments, x and y, and returns their product. Note that the arguments come before the colon and there is an implicit return of the expression on the right hand side of the colon.

The lambda expression creates a new instance of a function—mul:

```
>>> mul
<function <lambda> at 0x7fd6e694b9b0>
```

This function is *callable* and can be invoked by adding parentheses to the name:

```
>>> mul(3, 4)
12
```

This function is equivalent to the normal function, `mul2`, defined below, except that `mul` is slightly more succinct:

```
>>> def mul2(x, y):
...     return x * y

>>> mul2
<function mul2 at 0x7fd6e694b948>
```

Though both functions, `mul` and `mul2`, are distinct functions, they return the same value:

```
>>> mul(4,5) == mul2(4,5)
True
```

The `lambda` construct supports the various parameter types that functions support. A `lambda` expression can have zero parameters:

```
>>> one = lambda : 1
>>> one()
1
```

`lambda` expressions support named or default parameters as well:

```
>>> add_n = lambda x, n=3: x + n
>>> add_n(2)
5
>>> add_n(1, 4)
5
```

In addition, variable parameters and variable keyword parameters are supported in `lambda` expressions. As such, these expressions are able to accept any number of arguments if they are so designed.

The biggest drawback to `lambda` expressions is that they only support a single *expression* in their body. This severely handicaps their utility. They are commonly used for predicate functions, simple converters, destructuring of objects, and enabling lazy evaluation.

The Python Language Reference[†] explains that a simple `lambda` expression:

```
lambda arguments: expression
```

is equivalent to:

```
def name(arguments):
    return expression
```

Code that would belong in `expression` in the function above would work in a `lambda` expression.

Note

What is the difference between an *expression* and a *statement* in Python?

Expressions include arithmetic, unary, binary, boolean, and comparison operations. In addition list comprehensions and generator expressions. See the Python reference on Expressions[‡] for the BNF notation that describes them. An easy way to think of them is *something that can be returned*.

Statements are composed of simple statements and compound statements. Simple statements are a superset of expressions and also include assignment, calls to functions, `pass`, `del`, `print`, `return`, `yield`, `raise`, `break`, `continue`, `import`, `global`, and `exec`. More details can be found in the Python reference on Statements[§].

Compound statements include `if`, `while`, `for`, `try`, `with`, `def`, and `class`. These are detailed in the Python reference for Compound Statements[¶].

As an example, a `lambda` expression can have a *conditional expression* in it, but it may not have an `if` statement in it. A conditional expression (PEP 308) in Python is referred to as a *ternary operator* in other languages:

```
>>> is_pos = lambda x: 'pos' if x >= 0 else 'neg'
>>> is_pos(3)
'pos'

>>> is_pos2 = lambda x: if x >=0: 'pos'
  File "<stdin>", line 1
```

[†]http://docs.python.org/2/reference/expressions.html#lambda

113

Note (cont.)

```
    is_pos2 = lambda x: if x >=0: 'pos'
                          ^
SyntaxError: invalid syntax
```

Another common use of lambda functions is to determine the sort order of sequences. Both the cmp and key parameters in the sort method and sorted function accept functions to determine sort order. lambda expressions allow for easy inlining of these functions. An example is found in cookielib.py in the standard library:

```
# add cookies in order of most specific
# (ie. longest) path first
cookies.sort(key=lambda arg: len(arg.path),
    reverse=True)
```

Here, the in-place sort function is going to use the length of the cookie path to determine sort order. The reverse parameter is set to True, so that the largest sized paths come first instead of the shortest.

Note

Recommended practice for sorting is to use the key parameter instead of cmp. cmp is deprecated and removed from Python 3.

More real-life examples of lambda are illustrated by the sections that follow.

[‡]http://docs.python.org/reference/expressions.html

[§]http://docs.python.org/reference/simple_stmts.html

[¶]http://docs.python.org/reference/compound_stmts.html

> **Note**
>
> The `lambda` functions illustrated are *side-effect* free. Such functions are considered *pure* and enable:
>
> - Compiler optimizations (Python does not optimize them though)
>
> - Consistent composition of functions
>
> - A programmer to more easily reason about a function—that it is bug-free
>
> - Ease of testing
>
> - Can be executed in parallel
>
> In short, *pure* functions simplify programming. Functional programming encourages one to limit side-effect which can theoretically lead to better programs.

16.1 Higher-order functions

Another functional programming term is *higher-order function*. A higher-order function is a function that accepts (first-class) functions as parameters, or return functions as results. This construct enables composition of functions, invoking arbitrary functions any number of times or generating new functions on the fly. Also the built-in functional functions—`map`, `filter` and `reduce`—accept a function as a parameter.

Chapter 17

map

The built-in function map is a higher-order function that takes two arguments. It accepts a function and an arbitrary amount of sequences as arguments. If a single sequence is passed in, the result of map is a new list containing the result of the function applied to every item in the sequence. For example, the following converts a list of integers to strings:

```
>>> nums = [0, 1, 2]
>>> strs = map(str, nums)
>>> strs
['0', '1', '2']  # [str(0), str(1), str(2)]
```

The original list is unchanged (not surprising given that functional programming encourages immutability):

```
>>> nums
[0, 1, 2]
```

If multiple sequences are passed into map, the function is passed each corresponding item of the sequences as parameters:

```
>>> map(lambda *x: sum(x), [0, 1, 2]
...     [10, 11, 12],
...     [20, 21, 22])
[30, 33, 36]
# [ sum([0, 10, 20]), sum([1, 11, 21]) ... ]
```

The tarfile.py module in the standard library contains an example of lambda in combination with map. The TarFileCompat

117

class, used to implement the zipfile interface, has a method namelist that illustrates their use. It returns the names of the files in the tar file:

```
def namelist(self):
    return map(lambda m: m.name, self.infolist())
```

Note

In Python 3, map is not a built-in function, but a built-in class that when iterated upon creates the result. The following is example code from Python 3 illustrating the lazy nature of map in Python 3:

```
>>> type(map)
<class 'type'>

>>> map(int, '123')
<map object at 0x7f78772f17d0>

>>> list(map(int, '123'))
[1, 2, 3]
```

One caveat to map (in Python 2) is that it only operates on finite sequences. Because it creates a list to store the results, it will not work with infinite generators or iterators. An alternative function that works with these is the imap function within the itertools package. The imap function is lazy and creates an iterator rather than a list. In fact it behaves as map in Python 3 (imap is removed from Python 3):

```
>>> from itertools import imap
>>> imap(int, '123')
<itertools.imap object at 0x7f974be07150>

>>> list(imap(int, '123'))
[1, 2, 3]
```

Note

A *list comprehension* offers a superset of the functionality found in the map function. The original example

---

Note (cont.)

converting integers to strings could be done with the following list comprehension:

```
>>> [str(num) for num in [0, 1, 2]]
['0', '1', '2']
```

Even Python 3, which once threatened to remove functional constructs[||] completely, still uses map. The map function can be more succinct than list comprehensions as the platform.py module shows:

```
ints = map(int, l)
```

Whereas the list comprehension (discussed in detail later) version would read:

```
ints = [int(x) for x in l]
```

In addition, a *generator expression* also offers a super-set of the functionality found in itertools.imap and the Python 3 map class.

Chapter 18

reduce

The built-in function `reduce` is another common functional construct. `reduce` accepts a function and a sequence as parameters. It applies the function beginning with the first two items of the sequence and then applies the function to the results of the previous application and the next item from the sequence. This repeats until the sequence exhausts. An example makes this clear:

```
>>> import operator
>>> reduce(operator.mul, [1,2,3,4])
24  # ((1 * 2) * 3) * 4
```

In practice, most cases where `reduce` is used, the built-in function `sum` offers less code that is easier to read.

> **Note**
>
> In Python 3 `reduce` is no longer a built-in function. It is moved to the `functools` module.

The `csv` module in Python 2 incorporates a reduce statement that is not a sum. The class `Sniffer` tries to guess the delimiter and the quote character of a csv file. Inside of this class, the variable `quotes` is a dictionary that counts the amount of times a potential quote character is used. The `quotechar` is the character that occurs the most and is calculated by applying reduce to a lambda function that determines which of two potential quotes occurs the most.

A trick found in this code is the use of named parameters to pass in a third argument to a lambda expression. From csv.py:

```
quotechar = reduce(lambda a, b, quotes=quotes:
                     (quotes[a] > quotes[b]) and
                     a or b, quotes.keys())
```

Given that reduce is no longer a built-in in Python 3, the Python 3 version of the standard library reads like so (this code also works in Python 2):

```
quotechar = max(quotes, key=quotes.get)
```

Functional programmers can do creative things with reduce. One Clojure programmer suggested creation of a dictionary mapping keys to the square of their value using a reduce construct. Here is a Python implementation of that idea:

```
>>> def to_dict(d, key):
...     d[key] = key * key
...     return d
>>> result = reduce(to_dict, [{}] + range(5))
>>> print result
{0: 0, 1: 1, 2: 4, 3: 9, 4: 16}
```

In the above case, the sequence to apply the to_dict function to the sequence, it first needed to be primed with an empty dictionary.

Note

The above example is workable, but *dict comprehensions* (found in Python 2.7+, see PEP 274) accomplish it much better:

```
>>> result = {x:x*x for x in range(5)}
>>> print result
{0: 0, 1: 1, 2: 4, 3: 9, 4: 16}
```

Previous to Python 2.7 and the introduction of dict comprehensions (yes "dict" not "dictionary"), the following would have been the Pythonic solution:

Note (cont.)

```
>>> result = dict((x,x*x) for x in range(5))
>>> print result
{0: 0, 1: 1, 2: 4, 3: 9, 4: 16}
```

Dict comprehensions are slightly more legible than invoking dict.

Chapter 19

filter

The built-in function `filter` is another functional construct. This function accepts a *predicate function* and a sequence as parameters. A predicate function accepts a single item and returns a boolean. The `filter` function returns all of the items in the sequence for which the predicate function called on the item is true.

For example, the following piece of code will collect the items in the list that are positive:

```
>>> nums = [0, -1, 3, 4, -2]
>>> filter(lambda x:x > 0, nums)
[3, 4]
```

Here is another method from the `TarFileCompat` class that uses `filter` and `lambda`. It is used to return the entries in a tar file:

```
def infolist(self):
    return filter(
        lambda m: m.type in REGULAR_TYPES,
        self.tarfile.getmembers())
```

> **Note**
>
> Again in Python 3, one of the themes is laziness. `filter` was not dropped in Python 3, but was converted to a lazy class.

The `glob` module in the standard library contains another example of a combination of `filter` with a `lambda`. This module is used to *glob* files by using simple shell style patterns. In this case, any filenames that are hidden (begin with .) are filtered out of the results. A lambda expression is used for the predicate function to ensure that . is not the first character is. From `glob.py`:

```
names = filter(lambda x: x[0] != '.', names)
```

In addition to duplicating the functionality of `map`, list comprehensions also replicate the `filter` function. In Python 3, the `glob` module replaced this line with a list comprehension:

```
names = [x for x in names if x[0] != '.']
```

Modern Python favors comprehensions in favor of `filter`.

Chapter 20

Recursion

Recursive calls in Python are functions (or methods) that call themselves. Such functions tend to be straightforward. A drawback is that they also use a large amount of memory if the language is not able to optimize for them. Python supports recursion as seen in this Fibonacci example:

```
>>> def fib(n):
...     if n == 0 or n == 1:
...         return 1
...     else:
...         return fib(n-1) + fib(n-2)

>>> fib(10)
89
```

Python has an issue with recursive algorithms, because it imposes a stack limit that dictates the number of recursive calls a function may perform. Consider the following function:

```
>>> def call_self():
...     call_self()
```

Invoking this function should hang the interpreter because it keeps calling itself. (Normal recursive calls have a *base case* where the result is no longer recursive, which the above lacks.) But when invoked, the interpreter does not hang:

```
>>> call_self()
Traceback (most recent call last):
  ... Lots of lines like
  ... File "recursive.py", line 2, in call_self
RuntimeError: maximum recursion depth exceeded
```

Indeed the stack limit prevents this from hanging Python. This is considered a feature by many, but also a wart to those who would like to use recursive calls. Functional programmers coming to Python are used to recursion, and some call for *Tail Call Optimization*.

20.1 Tail call optimization

This is an optimization that applies to certain recursive functions where they call themselves as the last operation. The previous definition of fib was not tail call recursive because the result is the sum of two recursive calls. A tail call example[**] of the Fibonacci function is:

```
>>> def fib2(n):
...     if n == 0:
...         return 0
...     return _fib(n, 1, 0, 1)

>>> def _fib(n, m, fibm_minus1, fibm):
...     if (n == m):
...         return fibm
...     return _fib(n, m+1, fibm, fibm_minus1 + fibm)
```

Notice that the recursive call in _fib is the call to _fib itself. Languages that optimize for such recursive invocations are able to easily reuse the stack and conserve memory.

Many functional languages take advantage of TCO to eliminate the creation of a new stack with every recursive call. This optimization is possible by replacing the current stack variables with the updated variables that the recursive call would use. Indeed, Guido himself, wrote a blog post[††] describing this optimization and how a possible implementation might occur. In the end, Guido dismissed TCO on the grounds that it breaks stack traces, and does not believe that

---

[**]Inspired by http://www.seas.harvard.edu/hc3/bospre/facility/fibonacci/fibona

recursion should have a prime spot as a cornerstone of programming.

Another of Guido's points is that recursive functions are translatable to non-recursive iterative code.

20.2 Unrolling recursive functions

Recursive algorithms can be replaced with iterative solutions. The mental leap required is to recognize that recursive calls create a new stack with each call. By simulating that stack in code, the recursion is removed:

```
>>> def fib3(n):
...     stack = [0,1]
...     if n in [0,1]:
...         return 1
...     else:
...         while n > 1:
...             stack.append(sum(stack))
...             stack.pop(0)
...             n -= 1
...     return sum(stack)
```

This solution also happens to be quicker than the recursive solution. fib calls itself $O(2^n)$ times, while fib3 calls itself $O(n)$ times. fib3(50) returns almost instantly, while fib(50) ran for over an hour on my laptop before I killed it.

Throwing in a stack certainly adds some noise and increases the line count. The iterative solution is probably harder to reason about than the recursive solution.

20.3 Recursive tips

The Python interpreter comes with rails to protect against using too much memory by creating too many stacks. This number is defined in sys.getrecursionlimit(). By default it is set to 1000. This number can also be modified with sys.setrecursionlimit if needed. If you know that your recursive function might approach the default value your

[††]http://neopythonic.blogspot.com/2009/04/tail-recursion-elimination.html

options are to tweak that recursion limit or to rewrite the function in an iterative manner.

Chapter 21

List Comprehensions

PEP 202 introduced a syntax that offers a superset of the functionality found in both map and filter—the *list comprehension*. List comprehensions allow for the creation of lists in one line of code. Usually the same code written in an imperative style is a bit longer.

For example, creating a list containing the string representation of a list of integers could be done imperatively in this manner (the functional version was implemented in the map section):

```
>>> strs = []
>>> for num in [0, 1, 2]:
...     strs.append(str(num))

>>> print strs
['0', '1', '2']
```

The list comprehension syntax allows for strs to be created in just one line:

```
>>> strs = [str(num) for num in [0, 1, 2]]

>>> print strs
['0', '1', '2']
```

This syntax can be confusing at first. Understanding the construction of the list comprehension may aid in comprehending it (pun intended). There are a few steps to translate a list accumulated during iteration over a loop to a list comprehension:

- Assign the result (`strs`) to brackets. The brackets signal to the reader of the code that a list will be returned:

  ```
  strs = [ ]
  ```

- Place the *for* loop construct inside the brackets. No colons are necessary:

  ```
  strs = [for num in [0, 1, 2]]
  ```

- Insert any operations that filter accumulation after the for loop. (In this case there are none.)

- Insert the accumulated object (`str(num)`) at the front directly following the left bracket. Insert parentheses around the object if it is a tuple:

  ```
  strs = [str(num) for num in [0, 1, 2]]
  ```

One way to interpret this construct while reading the code is "return a list containing the `str` of each number in 0, 1, 2". Observant readers will note that this is essentially the map function.

List comprehensions not only offer the functionality of map, but also that of `filter`. To imperatively filter positive numbers from a list the following code would suffice:

```
>>> nums = [0, -1, 3, 4, -2]
>>> pos = []
>>> for num in nums:
...     if num > 0:
...         pos.append(num)

>>> print pos
[3, 4]
```

The same code written as a list comprehension is below:

```
>>> pos = [num for num in nums if num > 0]

>>> print pos
[3, 4]
```

Again, here is the construction method to translate the imperative code to a list comprehension:

- Assign the result (pos) to brackets. The brackets signal that a list will be returned:

```
pos = [ ]
```

- Place the *for* loop construct inside the brackets. No colons are necessary:

```
pos = [for num in nums]
```

- Insert any operations that filter accumulation after the for loop:

```
pos = [for num in nums if num > 0]
```

- Insert the accumulated object (num) directly following the left bracket. Insert parentheses around the object if it is a tuple:

```
pos = [num for num in nums if num > 0]
```

Note

A notation similar to list comprehensions is called the *set-builder notation*. It is commonly found in math and algorithm books. Here is a simple example:
$$\{x \in U : \phi(x)\}$$
This states: take all x that are in U, such that $\phi(x)$ is true. The Python version would read something like this:

```
>>> [x for x in u if phi(x)]
```

It is straightforward to translate this notation to Python using list comprehensions.

Note

In Python 2, the *control* variable of the list compre-hension (num in the examples above) shadows the num in the global scope. Upon execution of the list compre-hension, the control variable overwrites the previous definition. This is considered a wart and was fixed for Python 3.

In Python 2.3+:

```
>>> num = 100
>>> nums = range(-5, 5)
>>> pos = [num for num in nums if num > 0]
>>> print num
4
```

In Python 3:

```
>>> num = 100
>>> nums = range(-5, 5)
>>> pos = [num for num in nums if num > 0]
>>> print(num)
100
```

21.1   Nested list comprehensions

List comprehensions may be nested as well. Suppose you wanted to make a nested matrix like this:

```
[[0, 1, 2, 3],
 [0, 1, 2, 3],
 [0, 1, 2, 3]]
```

A functional solution may look like this:

```
>>> import itertools
>>> matrix = list(itertools.repeat(range(4), 3))
>>> print matrix
[[0, 1, 2, 3], [0, 1, 2, 3], [0, 1, 2, 3]]
```

An imperative way to create this is with two for loops:

```
>>> matrix = []
>>> for y in range(3):
...     row = []
```

```
...       for x in range(4):
...           row.append(x)
...       matrix.append(row)
```

A simple attempt illustrates simple nesting:

```
>>> matrix = [x for y in range(3) for x in range(4)]

>>> print matrix
[0, 1, 2, 3, 0, 1, 2, 3, 0, 1, 2, 3]
```

This creates a one-dimensional list that repeats range(4) three times. For a two-dimensional list the rows need to be accumulated in their own comprehension.

An individual row can be created with a single list comprehension:

```
>>> row = [x for x in range(4)]
>>> row
[0, 1, 2, 3]
```

With another comprehension these rows can be accumulated into a list:

```
>>> matrix = [[x for x in range(4)] for y in range(3)]
>>> print matrix
[[0, 1, 2, 3], [0, 1, 2, 3], [0, 1, 2, 3]]
```

Here is another example that illustrates nested list comprehensions as well as an imperative solution. The goal is to create the following matrix:

```
[[1, 2, 3],
 [4, 5, 6],
 [7, 8, 9]]
```

One imperative way to do this is the following:

```
>>> matrix = []
>>> for row_num in range(3):
...       row = []
...       for x in range((row_num*3), (row_num*3)+3):
...           row.append(x+1)
...       matrix.append(row)
```

The nested list comprehension solution looks like this:

```
>>> matrix2 = [[x+1 for x in range((row_num*3),
...            (row_num*3)+3)] for row_num in range(3)]
```

```
>>> matrix == matrix2
True
```

List comprehensions can be arbitrarily deep, so creation of n-dimensional matrices is possible. Opinions vary, but most agree that the imperative solution is more readable.

Chapter 22

Generator Expressions

A general theme of Python, as it progressed from version 2 to 3, is laziness. List comprehensions turned out to be such a useful idea, that a lazily evaluated version of them was desired. Hence the *Generator Expression*, released in Python 2.4 and described in PEP 289.

Generator expressions look very similar to list comprehensions, but the brackets are replaced with parentheses. The first example of a list comprehension:

```
>>> strs = [str(num) for num in [0, 1, 2]]
```

Could be written as generator expression:

```
>>> strs_gen = (str(num) for num in [0, 1, 2])
```

Generator expressions do not return a list, rather a generator object, which follows the *iterator protocol*:

```
>>> strs_gen
<generator object <genexpr> at 0x7fc7a53cbe10>
>>> strs_gen.next()
'0'
>>> strs_gen.next()
'1'
>>> strs_gen.next()
'2'
>>> strs_gen.next()
Traceback (most recent call last):
  ...
StopIteration
```

22.1 Generator (expressions) exhaust

This leads to one of the first differences between a generator expression and a list comprehension. A list comprehension returns a list—which is *iterable*—it can be iterated over many times. A generator expression can only be iterated over once.

> **Tip**
>
> Through inspection of an object one can divine whether it is iterable or allows just one iteration. An object that allows for a single iteration will have an `__iter__` method and `next` method (or `__next__` in Python 3). An iterable object will have an `__iter__` method, but no `next` method. Every time the iterable object is being iterated over, the `__iter__` method returns a new object—an iterator—that is good for a single iteration.

The method for constructing a generator expression is the same as a list comprehension, the only difference being substituting parentheses the brackets. To create a lazy mapping of integers to strings do the following:

- Assign the result (`strs`) to parentheses. The parentheses signal to the reader of the code that a generator expression is being used and a generator object will be returned:

```
strs = ( )
```

- Place the *for* loop construct inside the parentheses. No colons are necessary:

```
strs = (for num in [0, 1, 2])
```

- Insert any operations that filter the lazy items after the for loop. (In this case there are none.)

- Insert the lazily accumulated object (`str(num)`) at the front directly following the left parentheses. Insert parentheses around the object if it is a tuple:

```
strs = (str(num) for num in [0, 1, 2])
```

22.2 No need for parentheses

When a generator expression is used as the sole argument to a function, the surrounding parentheses are superfluous:

```
>>> sum(x+2 for x in range(4))
14
```

Yet if there are multiple arguments to a callable, Python requires that parentheses surround the generator expression:

```
>>> sum(x for x in range(4), 10)
Traceback (most recent call last):
  ...
SyntaxError: Generator expression must be
parenthesized if not sole argument

>>> sum((x for x in range(4)), 10)
16
```

22.3 No variable leaking

Unlike list comprehensions (in Python 2), control variables in generator expressions do not leak into scope, even after the generator has been iterated over:

```
>>> num = 100
>>> nums = range(-5, 5)
>>> pos = (num for num in nums if num > 0)
>>> print num
100

# Iterate over the generator expression
>>> result = list(pos)
>>> print num
100
```

22.4 Generators and generator expressions

Generator expressions offer a subset of the functionality available in generators. Some generators may be more readable as generator expressions. Here are three ways of filtering out negative items in a sequence:

```
>>> def pos_generator(seq):
...     for x in seq:
...         if x >= 0:
...             yield x

>>> def pos_gen_exp(seq):
...     return (x for x in seq if x >= 0)

>>> import itertools
>>> pos_map = lambda seq:itertools.ifilter(
...     lambda x: x>=0, seq)

>>> list(pos_generator(range(-5, 5))) == \
...     list(pos_gen_exp(range(-5, 5))) == \
...     list(pos_map(range(-5, 5)))
True
```

In this case the generator expression is slightly more succinct, though perhaps harder to debug as there is no way to step into it.

The `string.py` module in the standard library shows an example of a generator expression:

```
# Capitalize the words in a string,
# e.g. " aBc   dEf " -> "Abc Def".
def capwords(s, sep=None):
    """capwords(s [,sep]) -> string

    Split the argument into words using
    split, capitalize each word using
    capitalize, and join the capitalized
    words using join.  If the optional
    second argument sep is absent or None,
    runs of whitespace characters are
    replaced by a single space and leading
    and trailing whitespace are removed,
    otherwise sep is used to split and
    join the words.

    """
    return (sep or ' ').join(x.capitalize()
        for x in s.split(sep))
```

In version 2.4 and 2.5 of Python a list comprehension is used instead of the generator expression.

Chapter 23

Dictionary Comprehensions

As mentioned previously, PEP 274 introduced *Dictionary Comprehensions* and *Set Comprehensions* in Python 2.7. These are analogous to list comprehensions. To create a dict comprehensions, simply replace [and] with { and } and provide a key : value mapping for the accumulated object. Below is an example of creating a dictionary that maps a string to an integer:

```
>>> str2int = {str(num):num for num in range(3)}
>>> str2int
{'1': 1, '0': 0, '2': 2}
```

Dictionary comprehensions are not lazy and evaluate upon creation in both Python 2.7 and Python 3. They do not work on infinite sequences, which makes sense because Python has no construct of an infinitely large dictionary.

Unlike list comprehensions, dictionary comprehensions do not allow the control variable to clobber existing variables with conflicting names:

```
>>> num = 100
>>> str2int = {str(num):num for num in range(3)}
>>> num
100
```

As of version 3.2, the Python standard library does not have any examples of dictionary comprehensions, though there are a few obvious candidates. For example the global variable _b32rev in base64.py is defined as follows:

```
_b32rev = dict([(v, long(k)) for k, v in
   _b32alphabet.items()])
```

Using dictionary comprehensions would shorten it to:

```
_b32rev = {v:long(k) for k, v in _b32alphabet.items()}
```

Chapter 24

Set Comprehensions

Set Comprehensions are another nicety from PEP 274. Simply replace [and] with { and } in a list comprehension to get a set instead:

```
>>> {num for num in range(3)}
set([0, 1, 2])
```

Again set comprehensions are not lazy and evaluate immediately.

There are no examples as of Python 3.2 of set comprehensions in the standard library. A viable candidate would be the complete_help method in the Cmd class in cmd.py:

```
def complete_help(self, *args):
    commands = set(self.completenames(*args))
    topics = set(a[5:] for a in self.get_names()
                 if a.startswith('help_' + args[0]))
    return list(commands | topics)
```

Using set comprehensions would alter it slightly:

```
def complete_help(self, *args):
    commands = {x for x in self.completenames(*args)}
    topics = {a[5:] for a in self.get_names()
              if a.startswith('help_' + args[0])}
    return list(commands | topics)
```

It's debatable whether the commands line is an improvement, though the change for topics is.

Note

The scoping behavior of list comprehensions is warty in Python 2. Even though set and dictionary comprehensions are not lazy, they don't have access to outer state's local variables (unlike list comprehensions). As such the control variable is not able to clobber the variables in the enclosing namespace:

```
>>> y = "global/local"
>>> list_comp = [locals()['y'] for x in [0]]
>>> list_comp
['global/local']
>>> gen_exp = (locals().get('y', None) for x in
...     [0])
>>> list(gen_exp)
[None]
>>> set_comp = {locals().get('y', None) for x in
...     [0]}
>>> set_comp
set([None])
>>> dict_comp = {1:locals().get('y', None) for x
...     in [0]}
>>> dict_comp
{1: None}
```

Note that this is fixed in Python 3. The list comprehension above will throw a KeyError.

Chapter 25

The operator **Module**

The standard library contains the operator module which provides functions that implement operations in Python. Such functions come in handy when using functional constructs or list comprehensions.

For example, I recently needed to convert the values of an existing dictionary to strings. A simple comprehension failed because the assignment is not an expression and hence not valid syntax:

```
>>> data = {'cycle': 0}
>>> [data[key] = str(value) for key, value in data.items()]
Traceback (most recent call last):
    ...
  [data[key] = str(value) for key, value in data.items()]
                ^
SyntaxError: invalid syntax
```

Calling setdefault does not work either because the keys are already in the dictionary so they will not get updated by the call. Writing a function to call to update the value would work:

```
>>> def update_dict(d, k, v):
...     d[k] = v

>>> [update_dict(data, key, str(value))
...     for key, value in data.items()]
```

But given that functional programmers (or list comprehension programmers) like to cram everything into a single line, we need to look further for a solution. The operator module provides the equivalent of update_dict in a function named setitem:

```
>>> import operator
>>> [operator.setitem(data, key, str(value))
...     for key, value in data.items()]
```

The operator functions are especially useful for developers who appreciate reduce. The sum function could be rewritten with reduce in combination with functools.partial:

```
>>> import functools
>>> sum2 = functools.partial(reduce, operator.add)
>>> sum2([3, 4, 5])
12
```

A sampling of the useful functions found in operator include:

Operation	Function
a + b	add(a, b)
a - b	sub(a, b)
a * b	mul(a, b)
a / b	div(a, b)
item.foo	attrgetter(item, foo)
item.foo.bar	attrgetter(item, foo, bar)
item[foo]	itemgetter(item, foo)
seq[i]	getitem(seq, i)
seq[i:j]	getslice(seq, i, j)

The Counter class in collections.py in the standard library has an example of using itemgetter. This module redefines itemgetter on import with the following line:

```
from operator import itemgetter as _itemgetter
```

The Counter class acts like a dictionary that maps a key to the count of the key. The most_common method from the Counter class will return a list with the key, value tuples sorted by the most frequently occurring key to the least frequent:

```
def most_common(self, n=None):
    '''List the n most common elements and
    their counts from the most common to the
    least.  If n is None, then list all
    element counts.

    >>> Counter('abcdeabcdabcaba').most_common(3)
    [('a', 5), ('b', 4), ('c', 3)]

    '''
    # Emulate Bag.sortedByCount from Smalltalk
    if n is None:
        return sorted(self.items(), key=_itemgetter(1),
            reverse=True)
    return _heapq.nlargest(n, self.items(),
        key=_itemgetter(1))
```

Use of the operator module is very useful when programming in a functional style or using comprehension constructs.

About the Author

Matt Harrison has over 11 years Python experience across the domains of search, build management and testing, business intelligence and storage.

He has presented and taught tutorials at conferences such as SCALE, PyCON and OSCON as well as local user conferences. The structure and content of this book is based off of first hand experience teaching Python to many individuals.

He blogs at `hairysun.com` and occasionally tweets useful Python related information at `@_mharrison_`.

Technical Editors

Over the last 10 years, *Luke Lee* has professionally written software for applications ranging from Python desktop and web applications to embedded C drivers for Solid State Disks. Currently, he writes scientific Python applications for Blue-back Reservoir in Houston, TX.

His enthusiasm for Python is emphasized throughout his presentations at several Python related conferences including

Pycon, PyTexas, and PyArkansas. He is also an active member of the Houston Django and Python user groups.

Amjith Ramanujam has been programming for over 10 years in various languages. Python is currently his favorite language. He has an unhealthy obsession towards performance tuning and optimization.

He has given talks at DjangoCon, Utah Open Source Conference, PyCon and local user groups, and loves sharing any cool stuff he learns.

He works on the Python instrumentation team at NewRelic where they concoct creative ways to find performance bottlenecks in Python webapps.

Index